The Lean Business Management System

Lean Accounting: Principles & Practices Toolkit

Brian Maskell, Bruce Baggaley,
Nick Katko, David Paino
Edited by Susan Lilly

2007
First Edition
BMA Press

The Lean Business Management System

Lean Accounting: Principles & Practices Toolkit

BMA Inc.
100 Springdale Road #110, Cherry Hill NJ 08003 USA
Tel: 609 239 1080
Email: information@maskell.com
Web: www.maskell.com

Printed in the United States of America

First Edition
10 9 8 7 6 5 4

ISBN 978-0-9789760-1-9

Introduction

The first national Lean Accounting Summit conference opened its doors in Dearborn, MI in September 2005. The day before the summit started we had our first Lean Accounting Learning Leaders meeting, bringing together a group of people with knowledge and experience of lean accounting. We were there to discuss lean accounting issues and to share our ideas, our issues, and our vision. One major outcome of this meeting was a decision to codify the current methods of lean accounting into a single one-page document called Lean Accounting: Principles, Practices, and Tools. This small book is the outcome of that decision.

It took the team of "learning leaders" about 3 months to develop the Principles, Practices, and Tools showing the current state-of-the-art for lean accounting . The purpose of this book is to provide concise information on how to implement and use these lean accounting tools. We recognize that lean accounting is a lot more than a series of tools, just as lean manufacturing is more than the so-called "lean toolbox". This comprises the Lean Business Management System required to drive and support the lean enterprise. But it is still important for finance professionals, lean advocates, value stream managers, and company executives to know how and when to use the tools of lean accounting.

This guide is published for the third national Lean Accounting Summit (September 2007) and is dedicated to our friends and colleagues comprising the Lean Accounting Learning Leaders; Orry Fiume, Jean Cunningham, Jim Huntzinger, Norman Bodek, Robin Cooper, Fred Garbinski, Jerry Solomon, Mark Delusio, Bill Waddel, Bob Emiliani, David Cochran, Doc Hall, Jamie Flinchbaugh, John Coomes, Larry Grasso, and Michael Bremer.

Acknowledgments

Our thanks to all the lean accounting fellow travelers we have worked with over the years. Lean accounting as a discipline has matured. Companies all over the world are applying good lean practices to their accounting and control functions. There are many variations, but the result is the same. The accountants and financial people have taken their rightful place on the lean team.

We would like to acknowledge our debt of gratitude to the hundreds of people we have worked with over the last 10 years or more as we have together begun to pursue perfection within their company finance, accounting, and management systems.

The Lean Business Management System

Lean manufacturing is a tightly integrated system for delivering value to customers in a continuous flow, from order to delivery, while working continuously to improve the process. The organized value stream is the structure that underlies lean.

Because it is integrated, a lean system will resist a piecemeal approach to making improvements if they are made without considering the impact of changes on the system as a whole. In fact, attempting to implement lean approaches on a piecemeal basis (such as cell-by-cell) without an over-all understanding of how the changes fit into planned system performance usually will undermine rather than improve business results of the lean system.

We maintain that lean manufacturing cannot be sustained long term without lean accounting. Simply put: lean accounting is a discipline that applies lean thinking to accounting control and measurement of the value stream. Lean accounting embodies an approach that takes a "lean systems view" of measuring and managing the financial performance of the lean business. Lean accounting is itself lean.

This guide presents methods (we call them "tools") that have proven useful in managing value stream financial performance. Just as the lean manufacturing system resists piecemeal approaches to improvement, so a lean accounting system demands an integrated approach. Lean accounting tools are designed with feedback loops so lean operations can continuously adapt to continuous changes in the environment: within the company, among the competition, and in the market as a whole.

The diagram below shows how the lean accounting tools provide continuous feedback and foster adaptation.

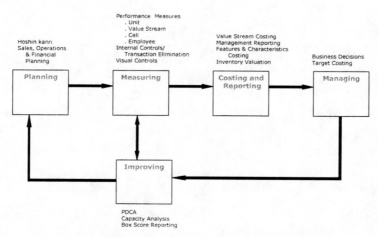

Figure 1. The lean business management system

Lean accounting tools are shown in the context of normal management functions: planning, measuring, costing and reporting (a special case of measuring), managing and improving. The over-all management system links business policy to external environmental change through hoshin kanri and target costing. These in turn affect what should be measured and improved (measuring and improving) and reported in the financial results (costing and reporting.) Improvements then feed back on the planning and measurement functions.

We cannot overemphasize the importance of implementing the tools we are presenting as a system, and not in a piecemeal fashion. For this reason we believe the accountant belongs on the lean team from the outset.

We hope these tools will give you what you need to support and sustain your company's lean implementation.

Brian Maskell, Bruce Baggaley, Nick Katko, David Paino, Susan Lilly
Cherry Hill NJ, 2007

Table of Contents

How to Use This Book

This Lean Business Management Systems toolkit is designed for you to use as a convenient and quick reference guide on the job. With some practice, you can put your finger on the tool you need efficiently and put it to work in your own business situation.

Do you already know what you need?

Use the Table of Contents. The sections are arranged in logical order, according to the principles, practices and tools map on page viii. Each part of the map is given a reference number. For example, there is a map section E2, "inventory valuation." E2 matches the chapter number within this guide where inventory valuation tools are described in detail.

Are you not sure what you need to use?

Use the lean accounting principles, practices and tools map to locate the area of your interest. This map organizes the practices and tools in different situations, and relates these to the principles of lean accounting. For example, if you're interested in "lean and simple business accounting" which is Principle A, you will find the practices related to this and the tools you will use to implement them on the map. The page number where that chapter/section begins is printed to the right.

Are you looking for bright ideas?

Look for our Suggestion Mascot in boxes like this throughout the guide.

Lean Accounting Principles, Practices, and Tools Map

Figure 2 on the next page summarizes the principles, practices, and tools of lean accounting. This map was developed by BMA Inc. in accordance with the vision of lean accounting developed at the Lean Accounting Summit, Dearborn, MI, September 2005.

Figure 2. The Lean Accounting Principles Practices and Tools Map

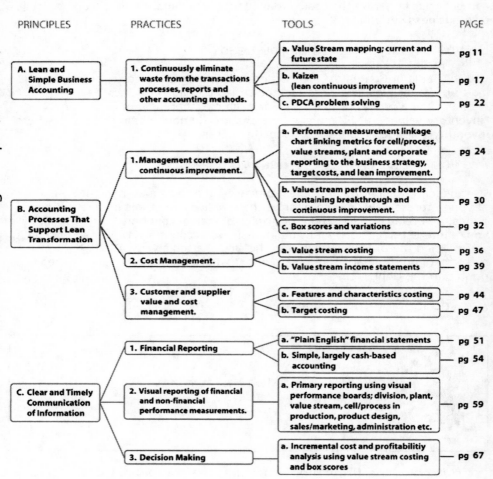

PRINCIPLES	PRACTICES	TOOLS	PAGE
A. Lean and Simple Business Accounting	**1. Continuously eliminate waste from the transactions processes, reports and other accounting methods.**	a. Value Stream mapping; current and future state	pg 11
		b. Kaizen (lean continuous improvement)	pg 17
		c. PDCA problem solving	pg 22
B. Accounting Processes That Support Lean Transformation	**1. Management control and continuous improvement.**	a. Performance measurement linkage chart linking metrics for cell/process, value streams, plant and corporate reporting to the business strategy, target costs, and lean improvement.	pg 24
		b. Value stream performance boards containing breakthrough and continuous improvement.	pg 30
		c. Box scores and variations	pg 32
	2. Cost Management.	a. Value stream costing	pg 36
		b. Value stream income statements	pg 39
	3. Customer and supplier value and cost management.	a. Features and characteristics costing	pg 44
		b. Target costing	pg 47
C. Clear and Timely Communication of Information	**1. Financial Reporting**	a. "Plain English" financial statements	pg 51
		b. Simple, largely cash-based accounting	pg 54
	2. Visual reporting of financial and non-financial performance measurements.	a. Primary reporting using visual performance boards; division, plant, value stream, cell/process in production, product design, sales/marketing, administration etc.	pg 59
	3. Decision Making	a. Incremental cost and profitabilitiy analysis using value stream costing and box scores	pg 67

Figure 2. The Lean Accounting Principles Practices and Tools Map (continued)

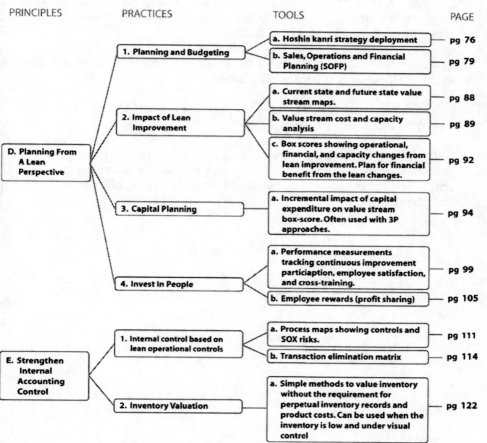

The Vision of Lean Accounting

· Provide accurate, timely, and understandable information to motivate lean transformation throughout the organization, and for decision-making leading to increased customer value, growth, profitability, and cash flow.

· Use lean tools to eliminate waste from the accounting processes while maintaining thorough financial control.

· Fully comply with GAAP, external reporting regulations, and internal reporting requirements.

· Support the lean culture by motivating investment in people, providing information that is relevant and actionable, and empower continuous improvement at every level of the organization.

BMA Inc. The Lean Accounting Leaders

A1: Lean Problem Solving and Continuous Improvement of Accounting Processes

Background

There are two major themes of lean accounting:
1. Applying lean to the company's accounting processes.
2. The lean business management system supporting lean thinking throughout the organization.

This section addresses the first of these themes. How do we make our accounting processes truly flow? How do we eliminate waste from the accounting processes? How do we make our accounting processes self-improving?

The simple answer is that lean thinking and methods are applied to accounting processes in the same way they are applied to other processes; whether manufacturing, engineering, sales and marketing, healthcare, retail, banking, or industrial.

The first thing we must do is to see the waste. For this we need to map the processes. The second is to have standard methods for creating lean improvement. And the third is that we must build of culture of continuous improvement leading to non-stop improvement.

The starting point for lean accounting is to recognize that all accounting, control, and measurement is 100% waste. There is nothing we do as accountants and controllers that adds value for the customers. This does not mean that our processes are unimportant -- indeed many of them are vital to the company's success. But it does mean that we need to work relentlessly to make these processes as little work as possible.

We are talking about the typical accounting tasks of month-end close, accounts payable, accounts receivable, payroll, and financial reporting. We are also including such processes as purchasing and receiving, shop floor control and work orders, inventory tracking, and other systems that are used for both operational control and financial control. We can, of course, gain considerable benefit from improving the month-end close, etc. But the real "heavy hitters" for waste elimination are the complex, transaction-based processes surrounding documents like work orders, purchase orders, supplier invoices, customer invoices, and inventory valuation and control.

In the early stages of lean accounting our efforts will be focused on improving these processes; reducing the waste, improving the flow, and cutting costs. As we progress, our primary focus will be on the elimination of the processes rather then merely improving them.

There are three categories of tools we apply to the task:
   a. Value stream mapping and process mapping
   b. Kaizen -- lean continuous improvement
   c. PDCA problem solving

We will treat each separately in this section.

a. Value stream maps and process maps

Value stream maps are commonly used to enable manufacturing people to understand the flow of production processes and to develop methods to improve the flow, reduce the waste, and cut costs. These same maps are also in a wide range of industries, such as hospital processes, banking processes, logistics processes, etc. The key to value stream mapping is that the map must show the entire process from beginning to end. This includes all the steps required to create value for the customers, and also includes a lot of steps that are thoroughly wasteful.

These maps usually include information about the accounting and support functions around the company's major processes, but they do not give a great deal of detailed information. In order to understand the flow and the waste in our accounting and control processes we need to map one level deeper and create process maps of the processes we are responsible for and need to improve.

What Is It?

A process map is a diagram showing all the steps in a process. Each step is documented with relevant information about the step including such things as the cycle time to complete a task, the rework or failure rate, the amount of disturbance time (or interruption time) for the people, system downtime, and other information.

What does it do?

The process map lets us see the whole flow of the process and identify where there is waste and where the flow is compromised. The map also allows us to use the information about each step to analyze the process, identify the amount of waste, and then understand what must be done to make improvement.

The primary purpose of the process map is to develop a "future state" process map showing the improvements we plan to make and a detailed action plan for implementing the changes.

Why use it?

The primary reason for these maps is to develop realistic action plans to improve the process, improve the flow, eliminate waste, and reduce the cost.

The activity of developing the process map with a team of people having responsibility to improve process is very valuable. It enables the team to share their knowledge and thoroughly understand the process as a group. It is common for people who have worked in the process for many years to discover that they did not correctly understand it, or that they had a limited view of the process because they understood only their small part of it.

Process maps show the "bigger picture". It is common with improvement projects that they are focused so closely to a small part of the process that -- while they may improve that part -- they do not improve the whole process very much. We need to have an understanding of the entire process so that our work does indeed improve the process and not just one small part of it.

Process maps are an excellent way to document what you are doing not only for the purpose of improvement but also for training, explaining the process to managers, and identifying key process steps required for such tasks as Sarbanes Oxley documentation.

How do I do it?

We urge people to draw process maps by hand on a large sheet of paper, flip chart, or "butcher paper" taped to the wall in the place where the process is performed. The team of people who have the responsibility for improving the process will draw the map. Post-It® notes come in handy as the team creates the map.

We use a five -step process to do this.

Step One: Assign an Improvement Team

This team will consist of 6-12 people. Most of the people will be subject experts; people having intimate knowledge of the process. It is likely that no one will have detailed knowledge of the entire process, so it is important that the team has at least one expert from each area of the process flow. The other members will include "customers" of the process, an outsider that can view the process with fresh eyes, and lean specialists to facilitate the improvement. The customers of the process will often be internal customers rather than the end customer.

Step Two: Start with the Customer

The starting point for mapping any process is the customer of the process. Identify the customer. Then identify what needs to be supplied to the customer by the process.

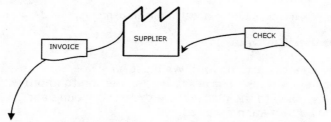

Figure 3. Starting point for mapping accounts payable

Let's take the accounts payable process as an example. The "customer" of the process is the supplier who needs to be paid. In this case the customer is also the primary supplier to the process; they supply the invoice that must be processed.

This example describes the accounts payable process for a central shared service within a large multi-national corporation. This department provides accounts payable processing for many different divisions and locations of the company. On average the shared services team processes 36,000 invoice lines each month and sends out a check for each of these.

Step Three: Identify all the Tasks within the Process

Working from the customer backwards, "walk" through the entire process and show all of the tasks required to complete the process. It is important that you physically walk through the entire process so that the team can see the process, understand the entire process, gather process data, and measure the process.

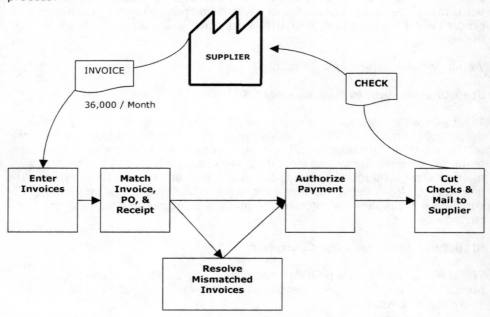

Figure 4. The steps required within the accounts payable department

Step Four: Gather the Data

All lean improvement is data driven. We must have valid and up-to-date data relating to the steps within the process we are seeking to improve. This data is best obtained by going to the place where the work is done and measuring or counting the key information required.

The next figure shows the data relating to the accounts payable process at our example company. The team has measured the cycle time for each task within the process, the rate of rejects in the matching process, and the number of documents that are in the queue at various places within the process. They have also measured the number of people in the department who complete these tasks.

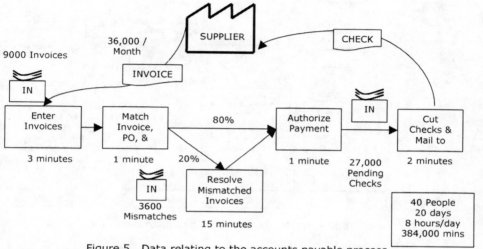

Figure 5. Data relating to the accounts payable process

Step Five: Analyze the Data

The next step is to analyze the data within the process and understand the process performance. The next figure shows the amount of time spent on each activity within the process and also the amount of capacity represented by the people in the department.

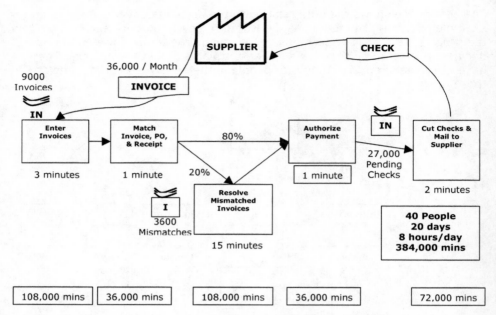

| 108,000 mins | 36,000 mins | | 108,000 mins | 36,000 mins | | 72,000 mins |

Figure 6. Time spent on activities and the department's capacity

The next figure shows a box score displaying information about the performance of the process. Operational measurements are in the top section; financial measurements in the lower section; and information about the use of the capacity within the process in the middle.

	Current State			
Flow time	22 days			
First time thru	80%			
Productivity	900			
Productive	66%			
Non-productive	28%			
Available capacity	6%			
Employee	$270,000			
Other costs	$100,000			
TOTAL cost	$370,000			
Cost / receipt	$10.28			

Figure 7. Box score for current state

Explanation of the box score:

Operational section:

Flow time; There are 39,600 documents in the queue within the process. The average number of documents completed each day is 1800 (36,000 in total in a 20 day month.) The flow time is 39,600 / 1800   = 22 days

First Time Through:

The number of invoices that flow through the process first time without additional manual validation is 80%. The other 20% go through the "resolve mismatches" task box.

Productivity:

The process requires 40 people and processes 36,000 invoice lines per month. The productivity of the process is 900 items per person (36,000 / 40).

Financial section:

This shows the total costs of the process. The 40 people cost $270,000 per month and other departmental expenses come to $100,000 making a total of $370,000 per month. The average cost per invoice is $10.28 ($370,000 / 36,000).

Capacity section:

The team made the decision that they would designate the capacity used "productively" within the process as the tasks in the primary flow which are: Enter Invoices, Match Invoices, Authorize Payment, and Cut Checks. The "non productive" capacity usage is the task required to resolve the mismatches. The "available capacity" is the time left over after the other two categories are complete. Here is how they are calculated:

Productive	(108,000 + 36,000 + 36,000 + 72,000) / Total Time (384,000) = 66%
Non-Productive	108,000 / 382,000 = 28%
Available Capacity	100% - (66% + 28%) = 6%

With this completed, the team is now ready to move into kaizen -- lean continuous improvement.

b. Kaizen -- lean continuous improvement

The word "kaizen" simply means continuous improvement. Continuous improvement is foundational to lean thinking and does not mean a series of projects to make the business better. It means that the organization develops a working culture whereby everyone in the company is engaged not only in performing their tasks but also in making daily improvement to their processes.

In order to remove waste from the accounts payable process our example team recognized that this would require a series of improvement initiatives. These initiatives would include methods to improve the flow and remove the waste from the process.   They also recognized that the process is complete waste and that their efforts should focus on eliminating altogether the need for the process. This is common with accounting processes. The early stages of kaizen concentrate on removing waste from the process, but as the company's lean thinking matures the emphasis will be on the removal of the process entirely. We use a five-step process to do this. Here's how our example company did this.

Step One: Establish a Team

Our example team established a weekly meeting where they studied the process, reviewed the current performance of the process, developed actions to improve the process, and reviewed the impact of these changes. During the week the team-members worked on their improvement tasks. This demanded the team members free up some time from their primary responsibilities in the accounts payable department to work on improvement activities.

Step Two: Develop Performance Measurements

The team set up a performance measurement board for the process. The performance measurement board showed the three primary measurements (productivity, flow time, and first time through) and the current state value stream map.

Team members gathered this data every week and also created pareto charts[2] showing the reasons for the problems within the process that caused lack of good performance. During their weekly meeting the team members worked to understand the root causes of these problems and established improvement tasks that were designed to improve outcomes by solving the root causes of the problems.

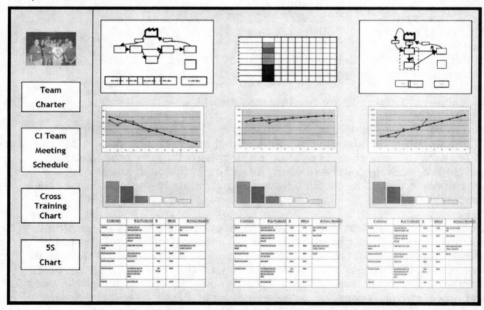

Figure 8. Accounts payable improvement board example

[2] See Memory Jogger II for an explanation of pareto charts. (The Memory Jogger II, Michael Brassard & Diane Ritter, Goal/QPC, Methuen MA , 1994.)

Figure 8 shows the Accounts payable improvement board. The board also shows the process maps, the detailed action plans for improvement tasks, and other relevant information.

Step Three: Develop Future State Process Maps

After they understood the root causes, the improvement team developed a future state map. The team created a vision for where they felt the accounts payable process should go over the longer term, but they quickly moved to practical changes they could accomplish in the short term. They then created a future state map showing the improvements they felt they could achieve over the next 3 months. Figure 9 shows the first future state map.

The team also developed a detailed action plan showing how these changes would be achieved over the next 3 months.

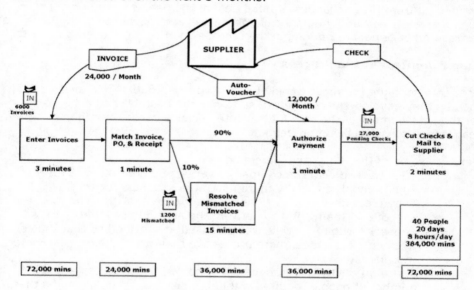

Figure 9.   Accounts payable future state #1 process map

Step Four: Implement the Future State

Achieving the first future state required converting some of the company's suppliers to auto vouchering, which permitted eliminating invoices for these suppliers. It also required making some improvements in the way purchase orders were raised to prevent some of the mismatches.

The results of these improvements are shown on the box score in Figure 10 (next page.)

	Current State	Future State #1	Future State #2	Long Term
Flow time	22 days	19 days		
First time thru	80%	83.3		
Productivity	900	900		
Productive	66%	53%		
Non-productive	28%	9%		
Available capacity	6%	38%		
Employee	$270,000	$270,000		
Other costs	$100,000	$100,000		
TOTAL cost	$370,000	$370,000		
Cost / receipt	$10.28	$10.28		

Figure 10. Box score for future state #1

You can see from the box score that there was considerable operational improvement from these changes. A good deal of the people's time (available capacity) was freed up. The financial impact was zero because we still have the same number of people working in the process and the same operating costs.

Step Five: Repeat the Process

The team continued to meet weekly to review their progress and every three months they developed a new future state map and established action plans for the achievement of the new future state. Over a twelve month period the team made considerable improvement.

Here are some of the things they implemented:
1. They worked with the company's various purchasing (or supply chain) people to certify more and more suppliers for self-billing.
2. They created cells where the people in the department worked together in teams of 4 to perform the accounts payable process.
3. The work within the cells was balanced and leveled so that the cells became a great deal more productive than when the people worked individually.
4. These productivity improvements enabled the team to reduce the number of people required within the process. After 9 months they were able to free up 18 people and by the end of the first year of work they free up a further 8 people.
5. The people freed up were moved to other positions within the organization. Some became value stream accountants working within the company's value stream to assist the value stream managers in cost reduction and reporting. Others moved into marketing and product development value streams working to better understand value creation for the customers and to build this into the company's products and services through the use of target costing. Others moved into various corporate responsibilities and lean improvement positions.

The process map at the end of the first 12 months of improvement is shown in Figure 11. The resulting box score is shown in Figure 12.

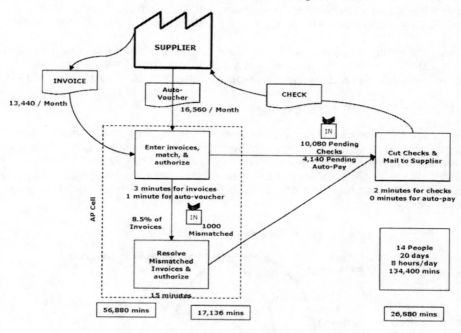

Figure 11. Process map for future state #4

	Current	Future#1	Future #2	Future #3	Future #4
Flow time	22 days	19 days	12.3 days	12.3 days	10.2 days
First time thru	80%	83.3	93.3%	93.3%	96.8%
Productivity	900	900	900	1636	2571
Productive	66%	53%	34%	63%	62%
Non-productive	28%	9%	9%	17%	13%
Available capacity	6%	38%	57%	20%	25%
Employee	$270,ooo	$270,000	$270,000	$148,500	$94,500
Other costs	$100,000	$100,000	$80,000	$70,000	$65,500
TOTAL cost	$370,000	$370,000	$350,000	$218,500	$160,000
Cost / receipt	$10.28	$10.28	$9.72	$6.07	$4.44

Figure 12. Box score for future state #4

In summary: there were no "silver bullets" that enabled the team to achieve these results. The improvement tasks include a wide range of initiatives to improve the flow, eliminate waste, address root cause problems in the operations processes, purchasing processes, administrative processes, as well as the accounts payable process itself.

The team continued to meet each week and continued to develop new process maps to drive further improvement, eliminate waste, and save cost. This work has been very satisfying to the team members. Prior to the company adopting lean thinking, these employees had never had any opportunity to take respon-sibility for improving their own processes. The department had operated for many years using the costly and wasteful methods of traditional management.

When you empower people and develop a culture of continuous improvement great things happen. The improvement of this accounts payable process was not a "project" -- it was and is an on-going culture of continuous improvement.

c. PDCA -- Problem solving

Lean continuous improvement is not done randomly; it is performed using formal problem solving methods. These methods are encapsulated within the Plan-Do-Check-Act (PDCA) system made famous by Dr. Edwards Deming in the 1980's. PDCA is often called the Shewart Circle, shown below (Figure 13) and named for Dr. Deming's mentor Dr. Shewart. See also Section D.1 for more about PDCA.

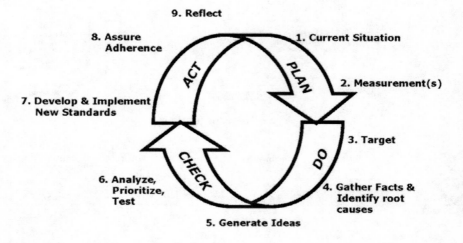

Figure 13. PDCA (Shewart) circle

The PDCA problem solving method provides a disciplined framework for problem solving leading to:

1. The solution of root causes rather than surface issues,
2. The application of the "scientific method" whereby improvement ideas are measured and results verified,
3. Demonstrated improvements are standardized and sustained,
4. Initial improvements lead to further improvement.

It is very important that lean continuous improvement is performed using these formal problem solving methods. Many companies have adopted the so-called A3 method developed within Toyota Motor Co. The entire problem is documented on a single sheet of large (A3 sized) paper containing a section for all the steps within the PDCA process. The format of these A3's varies considerably from one company to another. Figure 14 shows an example of A3 from the accounts payable processes discussed above.

ACCOUNTS PAYABLE A3   Achieve Future State #1

1. REASON	4. GAP ANALYSIS	7. ACTION PLAN
• The Accounts Payable process covers up problems and rarely lead to solutions. • Accounts Payable process is 100% waste. • There is opportunity to eliminate waste, reduce costs, solve root problems, and free up people for valued work.	• It will take many improvement steps to achieve the Future State. The Accounts Payable CI team can achieve improvement in flow and first time through over the next 3 months. • This will form a foundation for further improvement leading to the future state vision.	• Set up self-billing with Marshall (Week 2 JH/MM) • Establish pre-printed release forms with the value stream cost centers (Week 6 BM/SJL) • Obtain surcharge formula and include in PO release (Week 10 TY/FE) • Self Billing other 4 suppliers (week 12 JH/MM)
2. CURRENT STATE	5. SOLUTION	8. CONFIRMED STATE
• There is a large department – 40 people – processing 36,000 invoices a month. • As the company grows more people are required. • There is no formal problem solving or improvement process	• Bring 5 primary suppliers into certification and self-billing. These suppliers are already on pull systems. • Change Blanket PO release to eliminate most of the coding errors using pre-printed forms. • Pre-determine commodity surcharges so they are included in the released PO.	• Mismatched reduced from 20% to 80% • Self Billing reduced matching from 36,000 / month to 24,000
3. FUTURE STATE	6. RAPID EXPERIMENT	9. INSIGHTS
• The current workload can be achieve at 25% of the current cost using less than half the people. • The process can flow much better and create better relationships with our suppliers.	• Bring Marshall Inc. immediately into self-billing as they requested 2 month ago. • Use the experience from Marshall to apply to the other 4 suppliers. • If possible, include the other 4 suppliers in the work with Marshall.	• Supplier certification takes a long time and needs to be on-going process. Fewer suppliers would help. • Self-billing all primary suppliers will reduce invoices by 85% • It is possible over time to have all PO's with correct prices.

Figure 14. Sample A3 report for accounts payable

Variations

1.

Process maps can also be used for documenting Sarbanes Oxley (SOX) and ISO requirements and standard work. Most companies have created SOX documentation by writing large manuals and imposing standards on the process departments. Lean organizations have fulfilled SOX by drawing process maps, color coding the SOX risks, documenting the risk mitigations, and training the people using the maps and standardized work. This SOX documentation is often done during a lean improvement within the process. This way the documentation is a part of the overall improvement of the process. This approach leads to support from the process owners or value stream managers.

2.

There are many formats and methods for process mapping. It does not really matter which method you use. But make sure the diagram is easy to read and understand. Make sure you can "see" the flow. Make sure the required data is available and given on the map.

B1: Performance Measurements and Operational Continuous Improvement

Performance measurements in the lean system enable companies to adapt to changing conditions and obtain direct feedback about the effectiveness of continuous improvement efforts.

In a lean cell this involves indicators that signal a departure from standard work, standard time (takt) and standard inventory. If the lean goal is for the cell to get done during a shift what has to get done in the right quantity with the right quality, then anything that discloses a deviation indicates a problem in the lean system for that cell.

In a lean value stream this involves continuous adaptation to changes in the business environment and progress toward the planned future state. Performance measurements identify the need for change and help calibrate the effect of changes made toward goals. For the value stream, performance measurement is closely connected with continuous improvement.

We use three tools to develop and sustain lean performance management:

  a. The performance measurement linkage chart
  b. The value stream performance board
  c. The box score

a. Performance measurement linkage chart

What is it?

The linkage chart is a structured framework for focusing measurement on the factors that really count.   It helps the performance measures development team make sure the measurements they are putting in place are tightly aligned with strategic and value stream goals. By extending linkages through to the production process (cell) level, we also make sure these are properly aligned to over-all strategic and value stream goals.

What does it do?

The linkage chart provides the visual evidence that performance measures are in line with goals and critical success factors at every level of the lean organization.

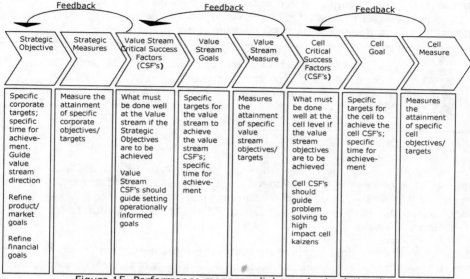

Figure 15. Performance measures linkage chart relationships

You can think of the linkage chart as a "big picture" tool. It serves to focus attention on the most important factors at the value stream level (value stream critical success factors) for achieving the desired strategic results (strategic goals.) It also throws light on measuring the most important factors at the cell level (cell critical success factors) and makes sure these are aligned with the desired value stream results (value stream goals.) Finally, the linkage chart sets specific targets at each level so progress can be measured as improvement efforts are implemented. Correctly done and linked, performance measures make sure the entire enterprise is operating in accordance with agreed-upon strategic objectives. Feedback travels up from the bottom as objectives are implemented, tracked and refined. At every level in the enterprise, factors or conditions critical for achieving success are disclosed and addressed.

1. Strategic objectives are matched with strategic measures: these are designed to measure the achievements of the business, as various initiatives are planned, deployed, and modified.
2. Value stream goals are matched with value stream measures: these primarily serve continuous improvement teams as they plan, deploy and evaluate improvement initiatives.
3. Cell goals are matched with cell measurements: these help the cell team calibrate their work and finish what needs to be done during the course of a shift; they also provide a common grass roots vernacular for identifying problems and developing countermeasures.

While the term "cell" suggests performance measurements for production operations, a cell in this context can also include support processes like purchasing, customer service, sales, quality, materials handling, accounting, and so forth. The examples given in this section focus on production cells, but the linkage chart is also used to develop local measurements for these administrative and support processes within the value stream.

 Post your linkage chart in a prominent place. As conditions change, revisit the chart. Ask yourself: are the risks and critical success factors still true? What else has to happen? When and why?

Why use it?

The lean company is tightly aligned operationally. Just-in-time production requires that cells adhere to standard work, standard (takt) time and standard inventory levels prescribed by the kanban rules. Immediate feedback of nonconformance with these rules is required at the cell level due to the tight operational linkages.

To sum up: use the linkage chart to define the most important things to measure, and then use this framework as a "living" tool to update measures and critical factors as conditions evolve in the business.

How do I do it?

We use a structured eleven-step process for implementing performance measures.

Step 1: Identify a value stream and cell within that value stream for the pilot.

This will test the method and prove out the usefulness of the performance measures by using them in an actual production setting. Pick a straight-forward manufacturing value stream that is clearly defined, has a relatively homogeneous mix of products and has few monuments.

 Pick a pilot cell where you have a good chance of success! Pick one where it's relatively easy to define what has to be produced each hour to meet takt and where standard work is defined. An assembly cell is often a good place to start.

Step 2: Assemble a team from the value stream and pilot cell.

This team will "own" the performance measures defined through the linkage analysis; they will manage the lean system you are creating. Performance measures will be created by team members themselves, not handed down by management. The team should represent a mix of the value stream functions, including value stream management, procurement, planning, accounting, material management and members of the pilot cell team. Keep the team to twenty members or less.

As you proceed with the team, make sure everyone participates. Be mindful that you are creating culture change. It's human nature: when people work together to create something, they are more apt to accept the outcome.

Step 3: Create a "wall chart" framework for the team to develop the analysis.

Here's an example:

Value Stream _____ Key Process _____						*Performance Measurement Starter Set*	
Strategic Objectives	Strategic Measurements	Value Stream CSF's	Value Stream Goals	Value Stream Measurements	Cell CSF's	Cell Goals	Cell Measurements

© Copyright MMA Inc. 2007

Figure 16. Performance measures wall chart example

Make sure to identify the value stream and key process (or cell.) We put this in the upper left-hand corner of the chart. This helps the team maintain focus.

If you can, laminate the chart. During the development process the team will be experimenting with alternatives. They can make changes easier without having to redraw the whole chart.

Step 4: Define the company's strategies for providing value to customers.

These strategies will define the ways the company wants to grow. The strategies you choose should relate to the value stream you have selected. Here are some examples:

Example #	Strategy for providing value to the customer	How you would measure this
1	Increase efficiency in the manufacturing and distribution processes.	Increase sales and cash flow from existing product sales to existing customers by ____ %
2	Increase efficiencies in the new product development and customer services processes.	Increase sales and cash flow from new product sales to existing customers by ____ %
3	Increase efficiencies in the sales and marketing processes.	Increase sales and cash flow from operations from existing product sales to new customers by ____ %
4	Increase efficiencies in both sales and marketing and new product development.	Increase sales and cash flow from new product sales to new customers by ____ %

Step 5: Relate goals and measures to the strategy.

Goals should be specific. They should specify, for example, how much increase in sales and cash flow is expected and by when.

Step 6: List and link (draw lines) the few things that the value stream must be good at to achieve the company's strategy.

These are your value stream critical success factors (CSF's). For lean companies these will always include being very good at the lean principles: namely creating value for customers; making the value stream flow at the rate of customer pull; perfecting the flow; and empowering people to define problems and become skilled in problem solving methodologies (such as PDCA.)

Step 7: Link the value stream CSF's to goals that will address them.

Usually, the value stream will have to achieve specific goals in productivity, on-time delivery, velocity (the time it takes to get through the value stream), cost per unit delivered, and first-pass yield quality. There should also be goals related to becoming better at lean. Once again these goals should be specific and state what must be achieved and by when.

Step 8: Develop measures for the goals and link these to value stream goals.

If the goals have been specific, defining measures for achieving them should be straightforward.

Step 9: List and link the few things that the cell must do to achieve the value stream goals.

These are your cell critical success factors (CSF's) Make certain these link to your value stream measures. Usually there are only a handful of things that the cell must accomplish if a value stream goal is to be achieved. For example:

BMA Inc. The Lean Accounting Leaders

if the value stream has to increase sales by 25%, then a cell CSF would be to free up capacity at the bottleneck to permit a 25% increase in volume. Remember, what must be done is always related to the actions that (if left unattended) would prevent the goal from being achieved.

Step 10: Develop cell goals linked to cell CSF's.

Once the limiting and enabling factors have been identified, cell goals can be precise. They should define the amount of change that will have to take place. In the example in step 9, cell production rates would have to be increased by 25% to enable an increase in sales of 25%.

Step 11: Develop cell measures linked to cell goals.

Once the goals have been defined, then cell measures can be readily defined.

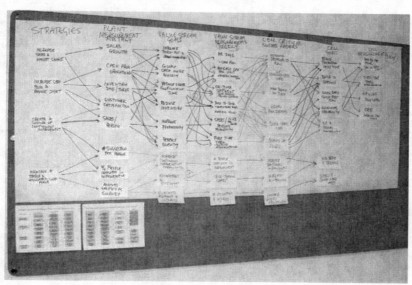

Figure 17. Example of a completed linkage chart

A graphical representation of part of a linkage chart:

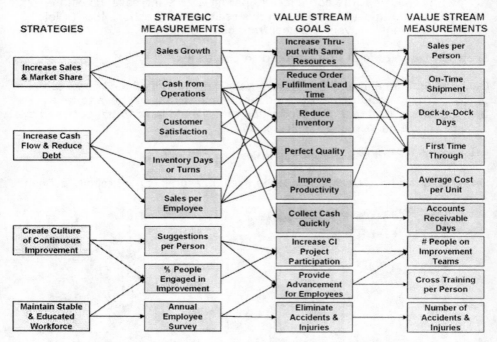

Figure 18. Strategic & value stream measurements for the order fulfillment value stream

b. Value stream performance board

What is it?

The value stream performance board is a visual display of progress toward business strategies and future state operations. It is used to manage and develop continuous improvement initiatives within the value stream.

The performance board should display at least four major components: trends against goals, analysis of factors critical to success, the status of improvement projects, and plans in the pipeline for breakthrough change.

When it comes to measurements, less is more. Too many measurements will cloud the issue. Right measurements properly linked to lean strategy will change behavior and create success.

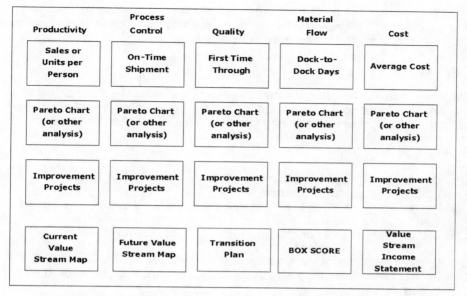

Figure 19. Schematic layout of a typical performance board

What does it do?

The measurement board provides the focus for weekly assessment of value stream performance including:

1. Progress toward planned results
2. Assessment of critical factors necessary to achieve the results
3. Design of high-impact improvement to affect the critical factors
4. Monitor effectiveness of improvement initiatives
5. Modification of initiatives as appropriate

There are two kinds of improvement displayed on the value stream performance board; break-through improvement and continuous improvement. The break-through improvement is shown on the current and future state value stream maps. The continuous improvement is shown on the value stream performance measurements, their related pareto charts, and the improvement projects emanating from the measurement process.

Break-through improvement is top-down improvement, developed from the value stream maps, and (generally) implemented using intense events (like a 5-day kaizen-blitz) completed by a temporary team. The result is radical change and improvement.

Continuous improvement is - in contrast - developed by the value stream team themselves. It is driven by the value stream performance measurements, and is completed by permanent improvement teams within the value stream. These improvement teams create significant change over time.

The value stream team members review the performance boards each week and ensure that the break-through improvement is on track as they coordinate the on-going continuous improvement projects.

Why use it?

The value stream performance measurement board lets the value stream team manage the continuous improvement program effectively. It helps focus improvement resources on achieving specific lean and the business goals.

How do I do it?

1. Create visual ways for displaying results and progress. These will include graphs, charts, and data arrays.
2. Provide thirteen-week trends of value stream operating results against value stream goals.
3. Display the progress of change/ improvement programs.
4. Display progress toward goals.
5. Display key value stream performance measures.
6. Update the display on a scheduled basis; be sure everything on the board is dated.
7. Post the display board in the value stream. Hold value stream team meetings around the board.

See also section C.2 on Visual Management.

c. Box score

What is it?

The box score is a concise report of the key operating, financial and capacity results of the lean value stream. There usually are a handful of measures that are important to the lean value stream (as developed via the linkage chart); put these in a box score and add it to the visual board.

The box score gives a 3-dimensional view of your value stream. It shows productive, non-productive and available capacity. On a single sheet you can see whether you are using your resources effectively and meeting goals.

		Current Value Stream	Remove "Low Margin" Products	Introduce New Products
		Jan-03	Jun-03	Sep-03
Operational	Units per Person	466	395	505
	On-Time-Shipment	92	99	99
	Dock-to-Dock Days	15	7	9
	First Time Thru	65	75	75
	Average Product Cost	$112.75	$120.94	$109.23
	AR Days	42	35	35
Capacity	Productive	24%	18%	28%
	Non-Productive	63%	35%	42%
	Available Capacity	13%	47%	30%
Financial	Revenue Monthly	$10,667	$9,866	$12,800
	Material Cost	$3,758	$3,185	$4,073
	Conversion Cost	$2,547	$2,547	$2,547
	Value Stream Gross Profit	$4,362	$4,134	$6,180

Figure 20. Box score example

This box score example consists of three sections showing planned and actual operating results, capacity usage and financial results.

Operating results section: Shows the impact of lean initiatives on value stream performance measures.

Financial results section: Shows the impact of lean initiatives on the value stream income statement.

Capacity usage section: Shows the impact lean initiatives on utilization of capacity, broken into three categories:

Productive capacity - the use of resources to convert raw material into finished product.

Non-productive capacity - the use of resources to create waste (change over, over production, wait time, machine downtime, rework/scrap, and the like.)

Available capacity - the amount of total available capacity remaining after considering productive and non-productive uses.

The box score is used widely in lean accounting. It is used for weekly summary reporting of value stream performance. It is used to assess the expected outcomes from lean improvement initiatives. It is used to develop plans for maximizing the financial benefit of lean changes. It is used for decision-making including make/buy analysis, pricing and quoting, capital investment decisions, and other times when there is a need to see the impact of change on the value stream as a whole.

What does it do?

The box score provides a way to gauge the effects of lean improvements on the three important dimensions of value stream performance: operating results, financial results and capacity usage.

Lean should improve operating results and shift capacity from non-productive uses to capacity available for growing the business. Thus, the box score is an important tool for planning sales and new product development programs to use the capacity that has been freed up by lean initiatives.

The box score is a key resource in making lean decisions about the value stream.

Why use it?

The box score literally puts everyone on the same page when evaluating results and planning changes in the value stream. Because it integrates the three aspects of the lean value stream, it provides a comprehensive view that is indispensable to value stream managers.

How to do it?

The data sources for each section of the box score are:

Operations	From the value stream performance measures; these are collected weekly by the value stream team.
Capacity	From the information contained in the data boxes on the value stream maps. Data boxes specify: 1. productive time for each operation (cycle time multiplied by quantity produced.) 2. non-productive time (percentage downtime, percentage rework/scrap, changeover time and batch size, and the like.) 3. available capacity is derived (total capacity minus (productive capacity plus non-productive capacity.) Capacity information must be recalculated each time a lean initiative is completed and the value stream map is changed.
Financial	From weekly sales and value stream costs and revenue.

The box score is a "living document" for planning the strategic and financial impact of lean and for managing progress toward planned results.

d. Box score variations

The Box score should be adapted to meet changing value stream conditions. For example, goals and critical success factors will change as business conditions, strategies and operating conditions in the value stream change. Companies using lean tools realize that they operate in a dynamic network of interrelated system elements, and seek to adapt them continuously.

Box scores that project into the future based on future state value stream maps, can help assess the pros and cons of alternative courses of action.

The frequency of review depends on the velocity of change in the value stream coupled with your company's problem-solving cycle time. In some cases this will permit monthly review. In other cases review must occur more frequently.

Some companies measure "capacity" only at the bottleneck operation; others measure all resources employed.

More examples of box scores and box score variations are described in the chapters on lean decision-making (section C.3) and visual management (section C.2.)

B2: Lean Cost Management

Lean cost management requires implementing two key tools that will optimize value stream managers' ability to understand the financial ramifications of lean changes. These are value stream costing, and value stream income statements.

a. Value stream costing (VSC)

Why use it?

Value stream costing (VSC) supports lean thinking and continuous improvement in the value stream. Traditional management accounting methods are usually actively hostile to lean manufacturing because they encourage and reinforce non-lean behaviors. VSC eliminates the need for these wasteful and misleading traditional systems.

What does it do?

VSC provides managers with cost and profitability information for each value stream. The attributes of VSC are:

1. VSC provides managers with cost and profitability information for each value stream.
2. Relevant, timely, actionable, and lean-focused information.
3. Financial reporting that everyone can understand.
4. Managers can closely control value stream costs.
5. VSC requires very little time or work because data is gathered as summary value stream direct costs.
6. Timely and accurate financial decisions relating to such things as pricing, quoting, profitability, make/buy, sourcing, and capital purchases, etc.
7. The true financial benefits of lean change and improvement can be shown.
8. Replaces standard product costing

How do I do it?

A value stream income statement is created every week for each value stream.

The revenue is the sales for the products manufactured in the value stream.

The costs include the materials used that week, outside process, employee costs, machine costs, facility costs, and other direct costs within the value stream. There is very little allocation because most of these costs can be assigned directly to the value stream.

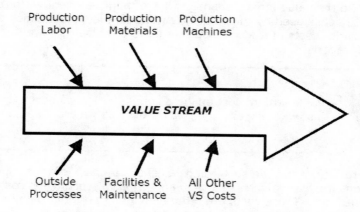

Figure 21. Classes of value stream cost

The people costs include the cost of all the people working in the value stream. There is no distinction between direct and indirect labor; anyone working in the value stream is considered direct. Most people are dedicated to a single value stream and require no allocation of their time. There is also no attempt to allocate costs occurring outside of the value stream.

Machine costs usually include the depreciation of the machines and any other machine-related costs such as maintenance performed by an outside maintenance contractor, spare parts, and utility costs - if they are significant.

Outside process costs are the cost of all the work done this week by outside contractors. If these costs are not invoiced weekly then the number and type of outside processes can be tracked so that these numbers are accurate without the need for an invoice.

Material costs include the costs of raw materials and purchased components used this week to manufacture the products. If the company's inventory is low (less than 30 days for example) then the cost of materials used will be the cost of materials purchased. If the raw materials inventory is not yet low and under control, then these costs may need to be tracked from issues to the value stream. These issues may be calculated using materials backflushing when the product is completed or shipped.

Alternatively, even if raw materials inventory is high, the materials cost can be gathered from total purchases but adjusted for the inventory change during the period.

Facilities costs are generally allocated. The total facilities costs are collected and the cost per square foot (or square meter) is calculated and allocated to the value streams. The value streams are only charged for the space they use; there is no attempt to fully absorb facilities costs into the value stream. Space includes factory space, office space, and warehouse space. Facilities costs are included so the value stream manager has a tangible incentive to reduce the amount of space used by the value stream. Some lean companies do not include facilities costs in the value stream costs because they want to completely avoid allocations.

> Value stream cost analysis coupled with box scores tells us not just what we are doing, but how well we are doing it!

Other direct costs include such things as shop supplies, office supplies, spare parts, consumable tools, travel costs, and other miscellaneous costs incurred during the week. These costs are often highlighted in more detail because they can be readily controlled by the value stream team; other costs - like machine costs - are more difficult to affect in the short term.

Most value streams contain "monuments". Monuments are machines or departments shared by more than one value stream. You should try to minimize them, but when there are monuments, it is necessary to allocate their costs across the affected value streams. Use a simple percentage allocation based on the activities of the monument. Avoid tracking the usage of the monument; usually a simple analysis at the beginning of the year is done to establish the allocation rates.

Value Stream Step	Materials	Outside	Employee	Machines	Facilities	Tooling	Other	TOTAL
Sales & Marketing			$10,150				$1,012	$11,162
Customer Service			$1,848					$1,848
Purchasing			$616					$616
Materials Handling			$1,576					$1,576
Part Fabrication	$63,544		$3,322	$1,529		$2,011		$70,406
Machining			$4,728	$6,584		$2,466		$13,778
Anodizing		$32,433						$32,433
Assembly	$47,887		$15,297			$366		$63,550
Shipping			$630					$630
Maintenance			$1,576				$101	$1,677
Product Engineering			$2,448					$2,448
Quality Assurance			$2,448					$2,448
Accounting			$816					$816
Managers & Supers			$4,060		$12,750		$2,177	$18,987
TOTAL	$111,431	$32,433	$49,515	$8,113	$12,750	$4,843	$3,290	$222,375

Figure 22. Value stream cost summary

When companies first organize by value streams they often run into the problem of having to share people across the value streams. The rule of thumb is to allocate these costs until they have been cross-trained to become dedicated to a single value stream. If you do not plan to cross-train and dedicate the people, then do not include their costs in the value stream costing.

b. Value stream income statements

The weekly value stream costs are used by the value stream manager to verify and control the costs of the value stream. The value stream costs are also used to create a weekly P&L (or income statement) for the value stream. Revenues for the products manufactured within the value stream are reported, the value stream profit is calculated, and the value stream's return on sales (or other useful factor) is shown.

Profit & Loss Report

	5-May-05	Per Unit	Percentage of Sales
Sales	$326,240	$173.90	1,876
Additional Revenue	$0		
Material Costs	$111,431	$59.40	34.16%
Employee Costs	$49,515	$26.39	15.18%
Machine Costs	$8,113	$4.32	
Outside Process Costs	$32,433	$17.29	9.94%
Other Costs	$16,040	$8.55	4.92%
Tooling	$4,843	$2.58	1.48%
Value Stream Profit	$103,865	$55	31.84%
ROS	31.84%		31.84%
Hurdle Rate	42.00%		
Cash Flow			
Inventory	$221,163	8.9	days
Accounts Receivable	$2,348,928	36.0	days
Accounts Payable	($624,014)	-28.0	days

Figure 23. Value stream income statement

The layout of the value stream income statement varies from company to company. It is most important to show all the direct costs but it is often helpful to provide more detailed information for the costs that can be directly controlled by the value stream manager. Some companies split the costs between fixed and variable costs. Others present the costs based on the flow through the value stream; procurement costs, conversion costs, distribution costs, support costs.

It is always important to show the history and trends associated with the income statement. These can be shown on the statement, shown graphically, or by using a box score.

Hurdle rate

It is common to assign a hurdle rate to a value stream. The hurdle rate is the minimum return-on-sales percentage the value stream should achieve. Hurdle rate is calculated by adding the required "bottom line" profitability percentage to the percentages of costs outside the value streams. These percentages often include the costs of non-value stream support people, product development value streams, corporate overhead allocations, etc. Figure 24 shows an example of this.

Required bottom line return	20%
Corporate overhead allocations	4%
Support costs outside value streams	8%
New product development value stream	18%
Hurdle rate for order fulfillment value streams	50%

Figure 24. Sample hurdle rate calculation

Advantages of value stream costing

1. VSC is simple to create, requires little work, and very few transactions. There is no need for labor reporting and other detailed job costing. The information is summary direct costing of the value stream; not the product or the production job.
2. VSC provides relevant and accurate financial information for the value stream manager and his/her team. The information is timely. Weekly reporting provides excellent cost control.
3. VSC focuses attention on the value stream: value stream issues, problems, and opportunities. This leads to value stream improvement and to teamwork, ownership, and accountability.
4. The financial information provided is easily understood by everyone: all the costs shown on the income statement are "real" and contain no complicated or arcane accounting methods.
5. VSC eliminates the need for standard product costs or other full absorption costing methods: as well as eliminating confusion and complexity, this also eliminates the misleading information stemming for standard costing.
6. The VSC reports can be developed each week by members of the value stream team: once the system is set up, it is not necessary for the accounting department to provide the information. It is readily available and straight-forward.

What must be in place for value stream costing?

1. Financial information must be reported by value stream, not by departments. This leads to a simplified chart of accounts with a lot fewer account numbers.
2. The value streams must be clearly defined with (most if not all) the people assigned to a single value stream, and limited "monuments" in the flow. Monuments generally derive from the purchase of large machines

from a mass production - rather than a lean - perspective. In the longer run these machines will be replaced by right-sized machines better suited for the value stream flow. But in the short term, monument costs must be assigned to the value streams using simple allocation methods.

3. VSC does not require that the value streams be excellent examples of lean flow, but the processes must be reasonably under control. Control requires that the processes are capable and that sensitive performance measurements (such as the cell measurements) are in use throughout the value stream.

See also section B.1.a. about performance measurements.

Variations

1. Seasonality: Many companies have significant seasonality in their value stream demand. This often requires setting a hurdle rate that varies from month to month or running the business based upon year-to-date information. Seasonality makes it difficult to use average costs based upon shipments. Average can be calculated based upon production quantities rather than shipment.

2. Value streams: There are no "perfect" value streams. Sometimes it is necessary to define "value streams" that do not provide any direct service to customers. These value streams are managed as cost centers rather then profit centers because they have no revenues. Sometimes one value stream serves another; for example a fabrication "value stream" (set up as a cost center) can provide components for more than one product family value stream. While this is an undesirable organization it is sometimes necessary. It is often unnecessary to pass the costs of these components across to the downstream value stream as this just requires transactions and may not provide any additional information.

3. Strategic decisions: Most tactical decisions can be made using the readily available value stream cost information and the income statements. Sometimes decisions require taking account of costs that are either outside the value streams or contained in more than one value stream. To achieve this, all the relevant costs are gathered onto a combined statement or a box score, and shown separately to give a clear explanation of the cost impact.

Value stream costing is for managing the business. Value stream costing makes (almost) all costs direct. If costs are direct, then cost and management accounting can be largely eliminated.

B3: Customer & Supplier Value

Fundamental to lean thinking are the following principles:

1. The purpose of the lean enterprise is to provide value to customers.
2. Value is provided through the value stream, which is a set of interconnected processes that transform a customer order to a product or service of value to the customer.
3. The most important feature of the lean value stream is the principle of "flow." Flow refers to the way the product or service travels through the process (manufacturing process, design process, service, healthcare, education, or other process) from order to customer at a continuous (or close to continuous) rate. This rate is the average rate (or takt time) at which the customer demands ("pulls") the product or service.

These principles demand answers to the following questions:

1. What is value to customers—how do we define this attribute and then measure the extent to which we are delivering it?
2. What do we mean by "flow"—how does that affect the way we think about cost and performance?

Simply stated, value is defined as: the set of product/service features and characteristics that satisfy a customer need or solve a customer problem, delivered when the customer wants them, and in the quantities and quality that the customer will pay for.

Customer value is why we are in business! Focus on producing customer value, not just on cost.

The second question: "How does flow affect the way we think about cost and performance?" demands greater explanation.

As the next diagram demonstrates, the cost of a product is related to its flow through the system. This rate of flow, in turn, is determined by the cycle time of the operation that is the longest.

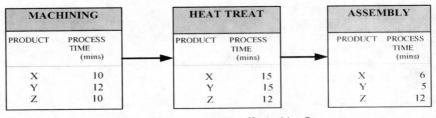

MACHINING			HEAT TREAT			ASSEMBLY	
PRODUCT	PROCESS TIME (mins)		PRODUCT	PROCESS TIME (mins)		PRODUCT	PROCESS TIME (mins)
X	10		X	15		X	6
Y	12		Y	15		Y	5
Z	10		Z	12		Z	12

Figure 25. How cost is affected by flow

Explanation of the example:

A value stream manufactures three products X, Y, and Z.

Each product goes through three cells, each of which has a team of people and machines.

Using value stream costing, we calculate the total conversion cost (excluding materials) of the value stream to be $1,000 per hour.

When the value stream makes Product X it can make 4 per hour because it is constrained by the heat treatment time of 15 minutes per unit. So the conversion cost of the Product X is $250 per unit ($1,000 / 4 units).

Similarly the conversion cost of product Y is also $250 per unit. Despite the fact that there is more labor and machine time required to make the Y, there are still only 4 manufactured per hour and the value stream costs are largely fixed.

Product Z costs less -- the value stream can make 5 per hour and the conversion cost per unit is $200 ($1,000 / 5 units).

We can see that the total time required to make Z is 34 minutes as compared with 31 minutes for X and 32 minutes for Y; but the cost of one Z is less than the cost of one X.

The cost of a product is NOT related to the amount of labor or machine time expended; it is based upon the rate of flow through the value stream.

Another key element: the entire process hinges on carefully interviewing customers to determine the product functionality that provides value then matching that with product features and characteristics that provide value. Later we will see how target costs can be defined for features and characteristics by matching their value assessments with their costs then initiating product redesign or process improvement as appropriate.

The implications are clear:
1. Product cost is not determined by the resources expended.
2. Product cost is determined by the rate of flow through the system.
3. Flow through the system is determined by rate of flow through the bottleneck work center.
4. Rate of flow through the bottleneck work center is determined by the product features and characteristics that consume the time of the bottleneck resource.

Therefore, product cost is always determined by conditions that (at a point in time) consume the bottleneck resource, including:

1. Product mix—some parts consume a great deal of resource time and some less.
2. Factors that affect availability—changeovers, downtime, waiting for parts, and the like.
3. Factors that affect quality as indicated by consumption of resource in making defective parts.

Discussion of product cost, then, must consider the ways in which product features and characteristics consume the bottleneck resource.

With this as background, we are ready to understand which features and characteristics provide value to customers. We can then use this as the basis for eliminating product features that consume a great deal of bottleneck resources but which do not provide value.

 Quality Function Deployment (QFD) identifies what customers value in products and services. Focus groups and careful surveys create understanding of the value proposition from the customer's point of view.

a. Features and characteristics costing

What is it?

Features and characteristics costing is a method for focusing on the factors that cause cost. It provides a simpler and much improved method for managing costs and sets up a framework for assessing customer value and cost associated with product features and variations.

The example below shows how features and characteristics costing works.

Assume a value stream produces brackets and struts for wing assemblies for the aircraft industry. These products had an average conversion cost of $100 per unit during the past month. Flow through the value stream is limited by the drilling machine cycle time, which during the prior month averaged 10 minutes.

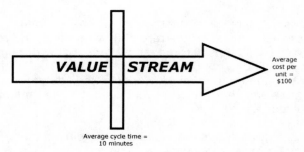

Average cost per unit = $100

Average cycle time = 10 minutes

Figure 26. The bottleneck operation is the drilling machine

The table in Figure 27 shows the cycle time through the drilling machine varies by the type of metal and the number of holes drilled per bracket. The time ranges from a low of one minute (to drill two holes in an aluminum bracket) and 100 minutes (to drill eight holes in a titanium bracket.) The time to drill four holes in a steel bracket is ten minutes and corresponds with the average cycle time through the drilling machine during the period.

Material

Number Holes Drilled		Aluminum	Steel	Titanium
	2	1	5	25
	4	2	**10**	50
	8	4	20	100

Figure 27. Processing variations based on product features

If this value stream only produced two-hole aluminum brackets, it could produce many more brackets in the same period of time than any other combination of features and characteristics. In fact, there could be one hundred times more brackets produced than if only eight-hole titanium brackets were produced!

This observation leads to the following extrapolation of the relationships of cycle time, volume through the value stream and average cost per unit. The table below is an array of the conversion costs for all products produced in the brackets value stream. The costs range from $10 for an aluminum bracket with two holes to $1000 with eight holes for a titanium one.

Material

Number Holes Drilled		Aluminum	Steel	Titanium
	2	$10	$50	$250
	4	$20	**$100**	$500
	8	$40	$200	$1000

Figure 28. Cycle time affects product unit cost

What does it do?

The features and characteristics costing method is a simple way to calculate the costs of a product based upon on an assessment of how its features and characteristics affect value stream flow during a defined period of time. While more accurate than standard costs, due to its greater currency, it cannot be used in decisions that apply to other periods of time.

Having said that, it is useful when a product cost is needed, such as in costing inventory, developing price lists and the like. Its primary advantage is its simplicity and its low cost to produce. Expensive computerized systems are not needed to produce detailed resource-based costs, because the features and characteristics approach serves just as well.

It is also useful in that it frees financial people from the time-consuming process of creating costs, and allows them to spend their time on the much more useful task of assessing cost causation, such as:

1. How features and characteristics affect product design.
2. How features and characteristics are valued by customers.
3. How to reduce costs and increase value through value engineering of products and focusing continuous improvement to free up the bottleneck.

How do I do it?

There are seven related major steps involved in figuring out features and characteristics costs shown below in Figure 29.

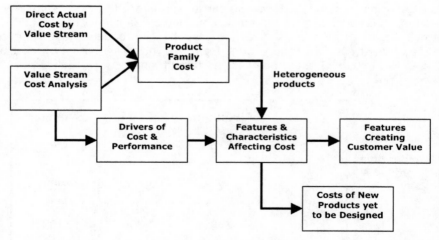

Figure 29. Seven steps for determining features and characteristics costs

The results of developing features and characteristics costs are applied to great advantage in target costing, which we cover in the next section.

b. Target costing

Target costing is a way to relate cost and value of a product or service features and characteristics to business processes.

The goal of target costing is to focus continuous improvement and product design on those areas that have the highest impact on reducing cost and increasing customer value.

What is it?

Value/cost relationships are driven from the economic requirements of the business, as shown in Figure 30.

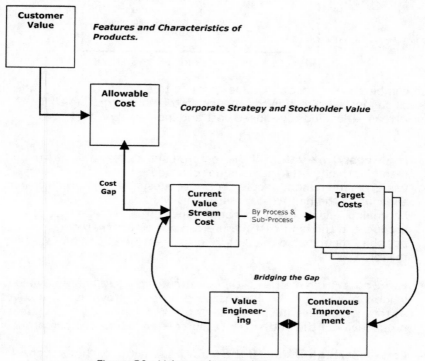

Figure 30. Value and cost relationships

Customer value in a competitive market drives pricing. As shown, this can create a "cost gap" between what costs actually are and what they must be ("allowable cost") if "required profitability" is to be achieved. This gap is closed by evaluating the cost/value relationships (using a 4-box diagram in our analysis below) of features and characteristics and designing continuous improvement efforts aimed at eliminating obstacles to value stream flow at the bottleneck.

The cost/value analysis for any feature/characteristic or business process is structured similarly to the following example:

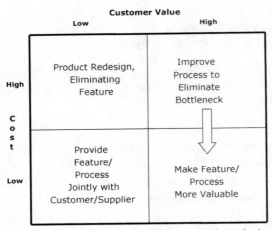

Figure 31. Customer value vs. cost analysis

Each combination of cost and value ascribed to a product feature and/business process suggests a direction for enhancing the value-creating ability of the value stream— leading to reduced cost and increased profitability.

- **High-cost/low-value:** If the feature uses a great deal of the bottleneck resource (high cost) and does not contribute to customer value (low value), management should consider redesigning the product and eliminating the high-cost feature. This will have the effect of improving value stream flow and reducing the average cost of all products. If the high-cost feature can not be eliminated, it may be possible to outsource the feature or process to a company specializing in this process.

- **High-cost/high-value:** If the feature is high cost and high value, the value stream team should consider process improvement initiatives (such as total productive maintenance or quick changeover) that increase the productivity of the bottleneck resource— or reduce costs in other ways.

- **Low-cost/high-value:** If the feature uses little of the bottleneck resource but is highly valued by the customer, then the value stream team should consider ways to build this feature into the customer value proposition, so as to preempt competition. If we can provide more of this feature and make our approach unique in some way, then we can provide very high value and uniqueness for our product.

- **Low-cost/low-value:** In this category are included processes such as inventory management, supplier accounts receivable and accounts payable—necessary processes under the existing structure but nevertheless not value adding for the customer. These should be considered for joint operation with customers and/or suppliers.

What does it do and why use it?

Understanding the value and cost relationship of product features and characteristics and of business processes is crucial to the development of new products and managing value on an ongoing basis. This analysis is crucial to:

1. Developing new products and processes
   a. Design to customer Value
   b. Target cost to design an effective value stream
2. Introducing new products into existing value streams
   a. Design to achieve maximum contribution from the value stream
3. Current products in current value streams
   a. Create more value and achieve target cost

How do I do it?

It is clear from the foregoing that properly evaluating features and characteristics and/or processes is central to effective application of target costing.

We use twelve structured steps to implement target costing.

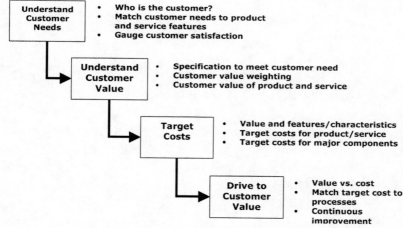

Figure 32. Steps for implementing target costing

These break down as follows:

1. Who is the customer? Understand the customer and what is of value to the customer.
2. Match customer needs to product and service features.
3. Find out how you are currently satisfying your customer.
4. Specify precisely how you will satisfy the customer in the future. Be clear and concise. This involves understanding what the customer needs in terms of such things as perfect quality, low price, short lead times and flexibility, reliable delivery, etc.
5. Decide how to weight the customer's values.

6. Link customer value to your products or services.
7. Link your value stream processes to achieving what the customer wants. Pinpoint exactly where and how in the value stream the desired value is created.
8. Link customer value to product features. Understand how value changes according to the features and characteristics of the product and service.
9. Develop your target costs on aggregate and on average in the value stream.
10. Use this analysis to develop detailed target costs for your key products. This will probably require a judgment call, taking into account lean improvements, new technologies, market changes, etc.
11. Match target costs to your process costs. This allows you to focus the continuous improvement teams to increase throughput and reduce cost. You may assign "interim target costs" if the cost gap is too wide as you get to work on improving the process.
12. Initiate continuous improvement activities to achieve the desired costs.

C1: Financial Reporting to Management

Value stream financial reports display the results of operations for each of the value streams within a plant. Plant financial statements consolidate results for all operations of value streams within the plant for a reporting period. Unlike reports prepared by traditional financial methods based on standard cost accounting, lean reports provide a clearer picture of the results of the value stream and other operations during the period. They are designed to provide the basis for taking action.

We use two principal tools for financial reporting to management in a lean company. These are:

 a. Plain-English financial statements
 b. Largely cash-based reporting

These tools are related, but we'll discuss them separately for ease of understanding.

a. Plain-English financial statements

Why this is important?

Traditional financial reports created from standard cost accounting often cannot be understood by management without a great deal of explanation by accountants. Unfortunately, most manufacturing companies report their financial results this way. People waste a lot of time just figuring out what the statements are saying. Instead of focusing on planning future actions, valuable time and resources are wasted. What is needed, especially in a lean company, is reporting that clearly states where the company has made money and why.

> Simple reports change the question ... from "What does this mean?" to "What should we do?" Accurate, timely, and actionable information is too important to lean success to waste time quibbling.

What is it?

A "plain-English" financial statement communicates financial results from operations in a way that is easily understood by non-financial people. It displays the primary reasons why current operations differ from those of a prior period.

Here is an example of a typical (not plain-English) operating report that would be presented to senior management. This lean company has two major lines of business, "OEM" and "Systems." The statement was created by subtracting cost of goods sold, calculated using the "standard cost," from revenues for the period to derive gross profit, and then applying a number of adjustments to achieve adjusted gross profit for the period.

TRADITIONAL INCOME STATEMENT

Revenue		Qty	per Unit	Total	
	OEM	18,300	$56.80	$1,039,440	51%
	Systems	9,830	$102.67	$1,009,246	49%
		28,130	$72.83	$2,048,686	
Cost of Goods Sold		28,130	$60.00	$1,687,800	82%
Gross Profit		28,130	$12.83	$360,886	18%
Adjustments					
Purchase Price Variance				($59,467)	
Materials Usage Variance				$96,733	
Labor Variance				($93,895)	
Overhead Absorption Variance				$182,577	6%
Adjusted Gross Profit				$486,834	
SG&A				$135,215	7%
Net Profit				$99,723	5%

Figure 33. Traditional income statement

The statement is surely accurate from an accounting point of view, but it doesn't communicate what is most relevant to management, namely: "Why were the profits for the period $99,723?" The answer is no doubt buried somewhere in the numbers, but where? And how? There are a number of basic questions that can not be answered from this statement. Among them:

1. How much profit was derived from "OEM" and how much from "Systems?" We can see the revenue, but which product line contributed more to the bottom line?
2. What are the components of cost of goods sold? (labor, material and over head) and how much did they actually cost?
3. What do all the "Adjustments" mean?

   - Why did we pay less for products during the period than standard, and is that a good thing? (purchase price variance)
   - Why did we use more materials during the period than standard, and what was the cause? (material usage variance)
   - Why did we pay less for labor to make the product and is that a good thing? (labor variance)
   - Why did we absorb less overhead than we should have and is that a bad thing? (overhead absorption variance). And what is absorption anyway?

The accountant knows that all the "adjustments" are required to transform cost of goods sold at standard cost to what was actually paid during the period. Of course, the accountant knows the standard costs were developed the prior year during the creation of the annual budget. But who knows whether a deviation from a standard, in either direction, is either good or bad? Furthermore, the "adjustments" are calculated based upon abstract conventions of accounting known only to accountants and are expressed in accounting jargon that has little relevance in common usage. Sure, the accountant can explain them, but is that how we want to spend our time in a management meeting?

Simple questions about profitability can not be explained by the statement shown, even after the adjustments have been explained. It lacks the right information to explain simply and understandably what happened during the period.

What does a plain-English statement look like?

The plain-English financial statement shown in Figure 34 displays clearly where profit was created during the period. It provides a concise guide to action for managers without necessarily any additional explanation by the accountant. It clearly answers the basic questions you can expect managers to have.

 Cost information is so important to lean manufacturing; you need much better ways to understand cost.

PLAIN ENGLISH FINANCIAL STATEMENT

	OEM Value Stream	Systems Value Stream	New Product Development	Sales & Marketing	Support	TOTAL
REVENUE	$1,039,440	$1,009,246				$2,048,686
Materials	$424,763	$339,810	$84,953	$0	$0	$849,526
Direct Labor	$189,336	$123,648	$0	$0	$0	$312,984
Support Labor	$87,662	$67,616	$40,772	$93,315	$53,056	$342,421
Machines	$88,800	$27,750	$0	$0	$0	$116,550
Outside process	$36,000	$17,731	$0	$0	$0	$53,731
Facilities	$15,450	$10,300	$3,090	$3,090	$9,270	$41,200
Other Costs	$1,933	$2,899	$483	$2,416	$1,933	$9,664
TOTAL COST	$843,944	$589,755	$129,298	$98,821	$64,259	$1,726,076
VALUE STREAM PROFIT	$195,496	$419,491	($129,298)	($98,821)	($64,259)	$322,610
Return on Sales	19%	42%	-6%	-5%	-3%	16%

Opening Inventory	$1,186,035
Closing Inventory	$963,148
Inventory Adjustment	($222,887)
NET PROFIT	$99,723
	5%

Figure 34. Plain-English financial statement

The statement in this example is from the same lean plant we visited in connection with our "traditional statement" above.

It shows precisely where the profits from the two lines of business (the two value streams) came from. But it goes further: it also shows the expenses that were incurred for other plant activities like "new product development" (which might include pre-production testing of new products, etc.) In our example plant there were "inside sales" activities. These have been broken out separately under the heading "Sales and Marketing." Finally, administrative activities such as general accounting, information systems, human resources and the like have been grouped into a category called "Support."

In contrast, the entire $135,215 of the sales and marketing and support costs were included in SG&A expense in our "traditional" income statement. But an additional $27,865 was "buried" in plant overhead costs and allocated by the accountants to units produced. Also, all of the $129,298 in new product development was lumped into overhead.

It is it any wonder why traditional statements are hard to understand and largely useless for lean decision-making?

On the other hand, the profit information on the plain-English financial statement is broken out by value stream. These are results that are directly controllable by the value stream managers. There are no allocated costs they don't understand and can't control. They will not need to waste any time trying to tease the importance of the reports from accountants in a meeting; the way is clear to make decisions going forward.

One key feature of the plain-English statement that stands out is this: the way costs are categorized. Notice they are broken out by resource type ("material" "outside processes", "facilities" etc.) Comparing value stream statements from period to period will clearly show the key differences. These can be explained by the value stream managers. No explanation by accountants is required. Resources included in the value stream numbers are limited only to those that were used by that value stream during the period. This means there are no costs that the value stream manager is not responsible for. **See also section B.2.a. about value stream costing.**

Finally, these statements are largely cash-based. This is discussed in the next section.

b. Largely cash-based financial reporting[3]

Cash-based financial statements are possible in a lean value stream because of the reduced time that products spend in the system and the stability of the lean processes themselves. Often, prior to lean, a product might remain in production for days, weeks or longer, but in a lean system this time is greatly reduced.

Cash-basis accounting greatly simplifies the preparation of financial statements on a GAAP (generally accepted accounting principles) basis. It also provides a clear picture of the financial effects of inventory reductions achieved through lean improvements.

[3] "Largely cash-based financial reporting" does not represent a change of accounting method. Lean accounting fully complies with GAAP and external reporting is accrual-based. Plain English income statements however show clearly the amount of cash spent during the period and do not confuse the numbers with allocations or opaque accounting methods for assigning costs. The result is the best of both worlds: fully GAAP-compliant accrual-based external reporting provided using statements that are clear and accessible to the managers who need them to run the company and make decisions.

What is it and why is it important?

Cash-based financial statements show the amounts of cash that have been expended during the period for operations. The following table shows what data is displayed, and where it comes from.

Cost Category	Basis	Source of Data
Materials	Voucher on receipt of Materials	Purchase journal
Direct Labor	When paid	Payroll system
Support Labor	When paid	Payroll system
Outside Processing	Supplier PO/invoice	Purchases journal
Machines	Depreciation expense	General Journal
Facilities	Square feet occupied	Standard Journal Entry
Other Costs	Voucher on receipt	Credit card payment

Figure 35. Data on the cash-based financial statement

Cash-basis accounting also simplifies preparation of financial statements, because most entries are generated from basic accounting records. There is no need to track detailed transactions through a complex computerized system to determine profits.

In a traditional system, when the length of time in process is longer and there is greater variability in production rates, it is necessary to track production in detail through a computerized system just to keep track of inventory.

Under the "matching principle" of GAAP, costs must be matched with the revenue earned through the shipment of products sold to customers. These costs are referred to as cost of goods sold. The costs for products made but not sold are "capitalized" on the balance sheet as "inventory," to be matched with future revenue. These costs are broken down into two categories:

1. Cash amounts for materials and other items purchased from outside suppliers. These costs are included in raw materials, work in process and finished goods inventories according to where they are in production at month end.
2. Labor and overhead paid for items that have not yet sold. These are "deferred costs", because they are capitalized on the balance sheet as work in process and finished goods inventories and will be matched with products sold in the future.

This requirement to match costs with revenue under GAAP compels the need for expensive systems to track production in detail.

On the other hand, when products speed through production more rapidly and when production rates are steady and level, such elaborate systems are neither practical nor necessary. Inventory is low and level, and can often be tracked visually. In this situation, cash expenditures can be considered equal to cost of goods sold under GAAP. There is no need for these wasteful tracking systems to create GAAP-compliant financial statements.

Another advantage of cash-based financial statements is that they are usually available quickly after the close of a month. They represent more current information, and can inform activities in the value stream quickly.

 I would rather know today that it costs $100 than wait three weeks to find out it costs $98.5603.

More importantly, for a manager in a lean company, traditional GAAP financial statements will show that the value stream is losing money when inventories are reduced. This is due to the deferred costs which were capitalized when inventories were high, but which show up as costs of the current period when inventories are reduced. This makes it seem that cost of goods sold is higher than it really is, and makes it difficult to understand the true effects of lean initiatives that cause inventory reductions.

The true beneficial effects of inventory reduction are readily apparent using cash-basis accounting. Material purchases are reduced and show up as reduced material costs in the cash basis P&L. All other costs continue and show no change.

How is it reconciled to GAAP?

The plain-English financial statement shown in Figure 22 is primarily a cash-basis report. Let's now explain how we reconcile from cash-basis profit for the plant to GAAP-basis profit.

The relevant portions of the statement in our example are reproduced below:

Value Stream Profit		$322,610
Opening Inventory	$1,186,035	
Less: Closing Inventory	963,148	
Inventory Change/Adjustment	(222,887)	(222,887)
GAAP Net Profit		$ 99,723

Cash-basis value stream profit must be adjusted for the changes in the inventory balances to arrive at GAAP. GAAP requires the prior period costs for material, labor and overhead that were expensed in the period be deferred on the balance sheet. When these become current period costs, inventory has to be reduced when they can no longer be deferred.

This becomes clearer in the analysis of cash basis and GAAP cost below:

Beginning Inventory		1,186,035
Value Stream Costs		1,726,076
Subtotal		2,912,111
Less: Ending Inventory		(963,148)
GAAP Cost of Goods Sold		$ 1,948,963

Note: the difference between value stream costs and GAAP cost of goods sold ($1,726,076- $1,948,963) is equal to $222,887—exactly equal to the reduction in inventory balances from the beginning to the end of the period ($1,186,035 - $963,148) or (in Figure 34) $222,887.

Other costs can also be shown "below the line". For example, larger corporations often allocate corporate costs to the divisions or plants. These costs may relate to centralized marketing, information systems, group-level administration, centralized "shared services", and so forth. These are usually arbitrary allocations that have no direct bearing on how the business is run, and can be shown as below-the-line adjustments.

C2: Visual Management

Background

Visual systems are used widely in lean manufacturing. Visual systems make sure the right things happen at the right time and that problems (which can inhibit flow or degrade quality) are easily and speedily identified and fixed. Waste is eliminated because there is no need to waste time and motion looking for tools, drawings and the like. The visual workplace is safer. The properly designed visual workplace is an essential foundation for creating standard work. Employees can focus on creating value for the customer. They become better team members, and also are empowered because they have access to information at every turn.

Visual systems fall into a number of broad categories; each category serves specific purposes in the lean workplace. These categories include:

1. Systems for sharing information
2. Systems for sharing standards and instructions
3. Systems for building standards into the workplace
4. Systems for raising alerts or alarms when needed
5. Systems for stopping defects
6. Systems for eliminating defects

Examples of these are shown in Figure 36.

Visual System Types	Examples		
1. Sharing Information	Cell signs Team photos Company news media story	Data in the computer Label on storage container HR programs	
2. Work Standards and Instructions	Value Stream Maps Standard Work Charts Visual Work Instructions	CI Project Boards VS performance boards Company mission and vision	Color coding machines by VS
3. Build Standards into the Work Place	Kanban cards Kanban Squares FIFO lanes	Shadow board Tool drawer with cut-outs for each tool Change-over cart	Waterspider "bus stops" Cell performance boards Floor markings for walkways
4. Alarms	Andon light Buzzers, whistles, bells "Magic eye" to prevent danger	Inspection process with a buzzer Forklift reverse siren	
5. Stopping Defects	Standard containers Sample products for comparison	Inspection that stops the process Guard rail	Odors added to natural gas Two buttons on a press
6. Eliminating Defects	Unique containers Redesign products for poka yoke	Clean room with access key	Governor on fork lift Tool drawer with unique slots

Figure 36. Examples of visual systems by type

BMA Inc. The Lean Accounting Leaders

"A visual workplace is a self-ordering, self-explaining, self-regulating, and self-improving work environment where what happens is what is supposed to happen because of visual methods." from "Visual Workplace -- Visual Thinking" by Gwendolyn Galsworth 2005

For lean accounting, visual performance boards are the method used to show how a value stream and its components (the cells, for example) are tracking against performance measurement targets and how the value stream is meeting its objectives.

See also section B.1.b. regarding value stream performance measures and using visual boards.

a. Visual performance boards

Why use them?

As we have seen, visual controls and signals are widely used in lean manufacturing to manage and operate the factory. From identifying the flow of materials to visual standard work, these signals and visual controls help people and teams see and react effectively to changing conditions. They keep production flowing and meeting goals. Visual systems of all types make it easy to see that processes are under control and performing correctly on the shop floor.

Visual performance boards perform analogous functions for performance and financial information. They quickly and clearly display the status of performance and promote a "management by seeing" approach. Performance measures are posted directly where the work is being done.   Management happens at the same place. Managers and finance people must get out of their offices and meet around the boards or walk through the factory when they are evaluating performance. This is a very important cultural characteristic for a lean organization.

The value stream board's primary purpose is to control the value stream. It addresses questions like: What do we want to accomplish? How are we doing? What are the problems we have, and what improvements do we have planned to correct them in our pursuit of perfection? Who is responsible?

The cell performance board's purpose is to help the cell team get done today what needs to get done, to serve the customer.

Figure 37. Value stream managers meeting in the factory
around the value stream board

What does the visual board do?

The visual boards support lean in the following ways:

1. They foster management by looking, seeing, and discussing issues on the shop floor (in the gemba) where the work is being done.
2. They help the cells get done today what needs to get done today (cell boards.)
3. They drive continuous improvement (value stream boards) by showing the current status of performance against goals.
4. They communicate all the information required for the day-to-day operation of the organization.
5. They provide rapid feedback for problem solving and continuous improvement activities.
6. They empower people by imparting knowledge that leads to real understanding and team building.

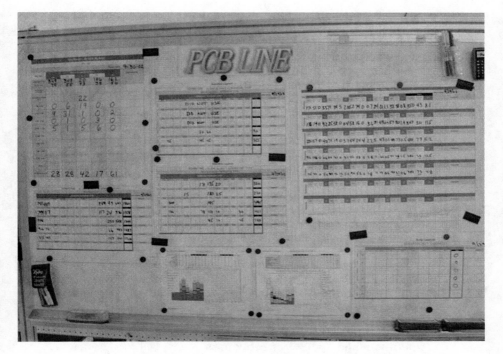

Figure 38. Example of a value stream board posted in a factory,
showing performance measures, such as downtime, on-time delivery, etc.

How do I do it?

We use a multi-step process to establish and use visual performance boards:

1. Establish the performance measures to be used. This involves using the performance measurement linkage chart. See section B.1.a. for how to identify the performance measures that you will use to control the business.
This step answers the question: What are we measuring? And why?

2. Design your performance board format and content, and assign responsibility for maintaining and updating the information. The data displayed should be simple and easy to gather, and it should be recorded by those actually doing the work. This gives the team itself ownership of the information, and provides "real-time" feedback. This step answers the question: How are we showing the measurements? Who is responsible?

3. Determine the "periodicity" of the boards; how often they should be updated. Make sure everyone understands the time frame related to the information. Make sure all performance charts carry reference dates. This answers the question: When do we change data? Daily? Weekly?

Generally, cell information changes daily; value stream information changes weekly, and plant information changes monthly.

4. Determine where the boards will be posted.
   a. Cell performance boards and support operation boards should be situated directly in the cell or office area where the work is being done.
   b. Value stream boards should be situated in a central area that allows easy access by everyone in the organization and guarantees good visibility. Somewhere physically in the value stream is best; in a back office is probably the worst choice. Depending on the organization, you may have several value stream boards and a location where the information is combined for the plant or site level. This answers the question: Where do we show our performance?

5. Make it easy to maintain the information. Have supplies, calculators, etc., handy. Visual performance boards are not "museum pieces." They are living management tools that people should see, understand, and act upon continuously. This answers the question: Are we doing all we can we do to foster a visual culture in the factory?

Typical cell performance measures we might see include:
   a. Day-by-the-hour
   b. First-time-thru
   c. WIP to SWIP
   d. Operational equipment effectiveness

Figure 39. Example of a cell day-by-the hour report

Figure 40. Cell "cube" contains all the measurements that control the cell

Value stream boards display value stream performance measures, which typically include operational and financial measurements such as:

1. Sales per person
2. On-time delivery
3. Dock to dock time
4. First-time-thru
5. Average cost per unit
6. AR days outstanding
7. Current state value stream map
8. Future state value stream map
9. Transition plan to achieve the future state
10. Value stream box score
11. Value stream P&L
12. Pareto charts or other priority lists of problem issues, projects for continuous improvement and the like

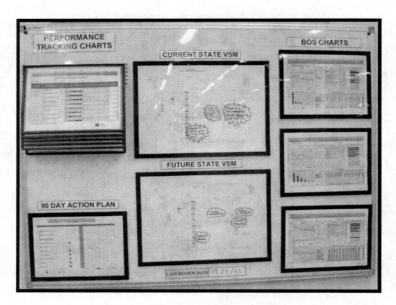

Figure 41. Value stream board showing performance,
action plans, value stream maps, etc.

See also section B.1.b. for details about how a typical value stream board
might be laid out.

Office boards and support measurements show the status of other critical processes.

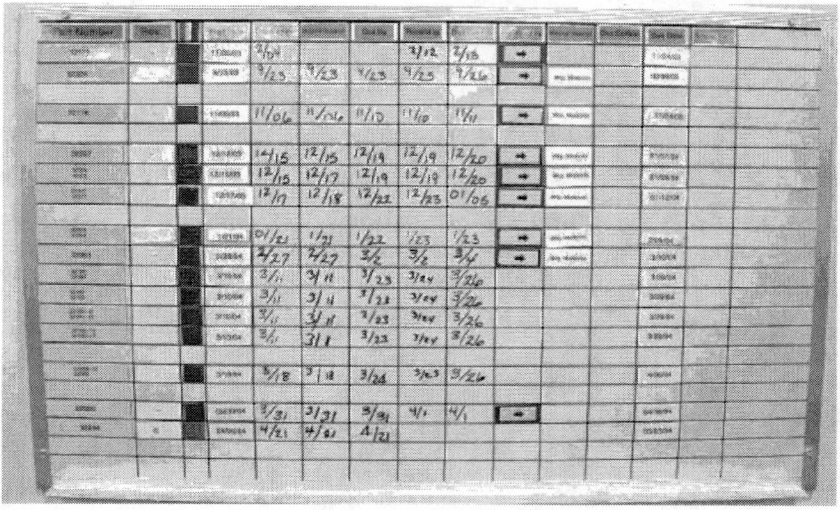

Figure 42. Board in engineering that tracks drawing approvals needed

Figure 43. Purchasing board, tracking supplier quality and performance

6. Supervisors, managers, and support personnel should perform daily "gemba" walks. Cell teams should meet around their boards every day and review what happened the day or shift before, what needs to be done today, and any problems that need to be addressed. The value stream team meets weekly to review the value stream board information, but they should also be involved individually on daily walks.

7. Performance boards become an integral part of managing a lean organization. Meetings move away from conference rooms and onto the shop floor and into the places where problems can be solved quickly. Teams at all levels are looking, seeing, discussing and taking action to make the business run better (continuous improvement) and meet customer needs (value.)

C3: Lean Decision-Making

Why use it?

The main reason for analyzing any business decision is to assess its impact on profitability.   Standard costing systems distort this analysis when they are applied in lean companies. We advocate using lean methods to make lean business decisions. Let's explain:

Background

Standard costing methods used to analyze business decisions are based on the traditional mass production manufacturing model. When a traditional company uses standard costing for decision-making, profitability decisions are based on criteria such as the impact on standard product margin and absorption.

There is nothing wrong with standard costing. It was developed by brilliant people between 1800 and 1925. But it was developed to support traditional mass-production, and lean manufacturing breaks the rules of mass production. Standard cost systems are the wrong tools for companies pursuing lean thinking.

The two methodologies could not be more different.

Traditional	Lean
Standard costs are calculated based upon fixed estimates of the amount of time and resources required to produce a product. Standard costs are usually set up at standard intervals (associated with budgeting) and often do not flex meaningfully with changing conditions.	Lean costs are calculated based on the time and resources required by the process. Lean costs may change due to changes in operating conditions, such as the rate of flow through the value stream as well as fluctuations in customer demand and product mix. In a lean company, continuous improvement means these factors will constantly be changing, making it impossible and/or meaningless to calculate a fixed product cost.
Standard costing assumes direct labor is a variable cost and there is a portion of overhead that is variable.	In a lean environment, labor is considered a fixed cost and is directly related to the capacity. In a lean company, it's more important to understand how that labor is used: whether it is used to produce for customer orders or is wasted on non-value-adding activities.
Most standard cost calculations attempt to use allocations to fully absorb overhead costs based on the amount of labor or machine time used to make the product. This results in too much overhead being applied to some products and too little to others.	Allocation is not necessary. Understanding how capacity is used is critical.

Using standard costs as the basis for decisions in a lean company virtually ensures making wrong decisions. Lean companies manage by value streams. Lean decision-making has to focus on the impact of a given decision on the value stream.

What does lean decision-making do?

1. Assesses the impact of business decisions on value stream operating performance, capacity and profitability.
2. Uses real-time, actual information to make decisions, rather than estimates or allocations.
3. Prevents the pitfalls of using standard costing in making wrong business decisions.
4. Focuses senior management and value stream managers on how profitable growth will be realized.

How do I do it?

We assess the impact of business decisions on value stream performance principally by using the box score. The box score is standard work for lean decision-making.

a. Using the box score to help make lean decisions

As we have seen, the box score displays the relationship between value stream operating performance, capacity and profitability in a succinct, usually 1-page format. Using the box score recognizes that these 3 dimensions of value stream performance are interrelated. Because of its unique format, the box score is especially suited for deciding among business alternatives. With this tool, decisions can be based on solid value stream-focused information.

Here is an example of a box score that shows the impact of removing low-margin items from production and introducing new products without increasing employees or making capital expenditures.

		Current Value Stream Jan-06	Remove "Low Margin" Products Jun-06	Introduce New Products Sep-06
Operational	Units per Person	465	395	505
	On-Time-Shipment	92	99	99
	Dock-to-Dock Days	15	7	9
	First Time Thru	65	75	75
	Average Product Cost	$112.75	$120.94	$109.23
	AR Days	42	35	35
Capacity	Productive	24%	18%	28%
	Non-Productive	63%	35%	42%
	Available Capacity	13%	47%	30%
Financial	Revenue Monthly	$10,667	$9,866	$12,800
	Material Cost	$3,758	$3,185	$4,073
	Conversion Cost	$2,547	$2,547	$2,547
	Value Stream Gross Profit	$4,362	$4,134	$6,180

Figure 44. Sample box score

Value stream profitability is directly related to demand, operating performance, and capacity of the value stream. The box score in Figure 44 makes this clear.

Putting it another way, the majority of value stream production costs (labor, machines and facilities) reflect how much is spent on capacity. The amount of capacity required is related to demand and stability of processes. Stable and reliable processes in a value stream (which will happen as lean manufacturing matures) allow a company to use more capacity for meeting customer demand, rather than on non-value adding activities. From a value stream perspective, revenue is related to demand, and cost management is a function of the amount of capacity required and the stability of processes. All three aspects of value stream performance must be considered when making lean business decisions.

To analyze the impact of business decisions, we want to look at the actual value stream P&L over a specified time period (a month, a year) rather than on a per unit basis, because it is largely impossible to calculate an accurate unit cost. The actual incremental revenue and costs resulting from the decision are calculated, and then the overall impact on value stream profitability is determined.

It is important for a company to understand its required value stream return on sales (ROS) and contribution margin in order to set minimum requirements. This can be accomplished by budgeting in a value stream format.

Standardized work in lean decision-making revolves around answering the following questions:

1. What is the impact on revenue?
2. What is the impact on costs?
3. What is the impact on capacity?
4. What is the impact on operating performance?

The following examples illustrate the lean decision-making process using box score information for some typical business decisions. A box score would be constructed using the elements listed in the column on the left, to answer the issues or questions indicated in the column on the right.

Box Score #1 Profitability of orders (order volume change)	
Performance measures: • Productivity • Flow • Quality • Cost • Customer service • Stability	What is the impact of the planned volume on performance and will this volume create capacity constraints? If demand has a negative impact on operational performance, then costs could increase.
Capacity • Productive • Nonproductive • Available	Is there available capacity to produce this volume?
Revenue	Price -- set by the customer Volume -- what is the required demand in units over the time period?
Material	Calculate actual cost from bill of material.
Production Costs • Labor • Machines • Facilities • Other	Is capacity available to produce this volume over the time period? If yes, then there are no additional production costs. If capacity is not available, then calculate the cost of capacity required -- additional labor (full-time, temporary, overtime), machines, facilities, etc. Also consider increase in costs due to negative operational performance.
Value stream profit	Does the ROS of the order(s) meet or exceed the target ROS?

		Current	6 Months	1 Year	18 Months	2 Years	30 Months	3 Years
	Additional Monthly Quantity	0	1	5	10	15	20	30
OPER-ATIONAL	Units per Person	1.52	1.54	1.63	1.80	1.90	2.16	2.59
	On-Time Shipment	100%	100%	100%	100%	100%	100%	100%
	Dock-to-Dock Days	6.0	6.0	6.0	5.0	5.0	4.5	4.5
	First Time Through	80	80%	85	85	85	85	85
	Average Product Cost	$3,481	$3,480	$3,278	$2,985	$2,821	$2,497	$2,092
	AR Days	42	42	42	42	37	37	37
CAPA-CITY	Productive	29%	33%	38%	34%	36%	41%	50%
	Non-Productive	54%	52%	55%	35%	33%	33%	33%
	Available	17%	15%	7%	31%	31%	26%	17%
FINAN-CIAL	Revenue	$466,670	$472,670	$502,568	$562,461	$630,17	$714,13	$834,172
	Material Costs	$172,085	$175,385	$178,685	$181,935	$184,686	$187,101	$189,160
	Conversion Costs	$119,584	$119,584	$119,584	$142,584	$142,584	$152,593	$158,084
	Value Stream Gross	$175,001	$177,701	$204,299	$237,942	$302,900	$374,438	$486,928
	Value Stream ROS	37.50%	37.60%	40.65%	42.30%	48.07%	52.43%	58.37%
	Additional People				5		2	1
	Additional Machines				3		2	1
	Material Costs per Unit		$3,300	$3,300	$3,250	$2,750	$2,325	$2,150

Figure 45. Box score showing the introduction of a new product family. New machines and additional people are required.

Box Score #3 Outsourcing existing production (This will reduce the demand in the value stream which will result in more available capacity.)	
Performance measures: • Productivity • Flow • Quality • Cost • Customer service • Stability	What is the impact of this reduction in volume on performance?
Capacity • Productive • Nonproductive • Available	• How much capacity will be created due to the reduction in volume? • What will be done with the available capacity? • Is there other demand which can use this newly created available capacity?
Revenue	If other demand can use available capacity, calculate revenue
Material	Calculate the difference between the actual cost of purchasing raw materials used in production and the actual cost of purchasing from a supplier; also calculate additional material cost of additional revenue
Production Costs • Labor • Machines • Facilities • Other	Production costs do not decrease unless the available capacity is transferred out of the value stream
Value stream profit	Does the ROS of the plan meet or exceed the target ROS?

		CURRENT STATE	OUTSOURCE LOCALLY	OUTSOURCE TO CHINA	MAKE IN-HOUSE
Operations	Productivity (Sales/person)	$8,689	$9,814	$9,814	$9,653
	On-Time Shipment	94.5%	92.5%	89.0%	95.0%
	Inventory Turns	12.25	11.19	11.12	12.44
	Average Cost	$25.53	$26.60	$26.10	$25.50
	Rejects Parts per Million	1250	3200	7500	1100
Capacity	Productive Capacity	42.0%	42.0%	42.0%	44.0%
	Non-Productive Capacity	45.0%	46.0%	49.0%	43.0%
	Available Capacity	13.0%	12.0%	9.0%	13.0%
Financial	Revenue	$1,042,631	$1,177,631	$1,177,631	$1,177,631
	Material Costs	$424,763	$538,763	$521,513	$491,753
	Conversion Costs	$392,089	$392,089	$392,089	$400,756
	Value Stream Profit	$225,779	$246,779	$264,029	$285,122
	Return on Sales	22%	21%	22%	24%

Figure 46. Box score - different sourcing options

Box Score #4 Capital purchases (also applies to hiring people)	
Performance measures: • Productivity • Flow • Quality • Cost • Customer service • Stability	What is the specific impact of the asset on operational performance?
Capacity • Productive • Nonproductive • Available	How much capacity will the asset create in the value stream? Is that capacity needed to meet demand?
Revenue	If asset's capacity is used to meet demand that otherwise cannot be met, calculate additional revenue
Material	Calculate material cost of additional revenue
Production Costs • Labor • Machines • Facilities • Other	Increase depreciation expense for the purchase of the asset Consider other costs which may change due to the purchase of the asset or operational improvements created by the asset
Value stream profit	Does the ROS meet or exceed the target ROS?

Box Score #5 Pricing and profitability	
Performance measures: • Productivity • Flow • Quality • Cost • Customer Service • Stability	
Capacity • Productive • Nonproductive • Available	
Revenue	Price -- set by the customer based on value derived from product Volume -- what is the projected volume?
Material	Use value engineering to reduce material cost to achieve required ROS
Production Costs • Labor • Machines • Facilities • Other	Use Target Costing to reduce production costs to achieve required ROS
Value stream profit	What is the company's required minimum ROS?

Box Score #6 Impact of continuous improvement	
Performance measures: • Productivity • Flow • Quality • Cost • Customer service • Stability	Project the future state of operational performance measures after continuous improvement.
Capacity • Productive • Nonproductive • Available	• Calculate future state capacity -- reduction in nonproductive and creation of available and/or productive • Is there other demand which can use this newly created available capacity?
Revenue	If demand exists, calculate revenue of this demand
Material	Calculate the actual cost of material for this demand
Production Costs • Labor • Machines • Facilities • Other	Calculate the reduction in actual costs due to continuous improvement (e.g. reduction in overtime, scrap, etc)
Value stream profit	Calculated. What will be the future impact on profit?

		13-Jun	20-Jun	27-Jun	4-Jul	11-Jul	18-Jul	25-Jul	1-Aug	15-Aug	FUTURE STATE
Operational	Units Per Person	15.18	15.63	14.7	15.91	15.9	16.59				20.7
	On-Time-Shipment	100%	100%	100%	100%	100%	100%				100%
	Dock-to-Dock Days	6.00	5.83	6.38	5.54	6.00	5.75				5.00
	First Time Thru	80%	80%	80%	85%	85%	85%				85%
	Average Product Cost	$343	$337	$362	$338	$337	$325				$262
	AR Days	42	42	42	42	37	37				37
Capacity	Productive	29%	29%	29%	28%	28%	28%				40%
	Non-Productive	54%	54%	54%	52%	52%	52%				33%
	Available Capacity	17%	17%	17%	20%	20%	20%				27%
Financial	Revenue	$470,900	$484,750	$455,942	$490,050	$487,910	$525,635				$576,375
	Material Cost	$172,085	$175,385	$178,685	$181,935	$184,685	$187,010				$189,160
	Conversion Cost	$179,231	$189,781	$119,584	$119,584	$142,584	$152,584				$158,084
	Value Stream Gross Profit	$179,231	$189,781	$157,673	$188,531	$160,641	$186,041				$229,131
	ROS	38.06%	39.15%	34.58%	38.47%	32.92%	35.39%				39.75%

Figure 47. Box score for weekly value stream reporting

		CURRENT STATE	FUTURE STATE	REMOVE UNNEEDED future state 2	INCREASE SALES future state 3	INSOURCE SUB-ASSY future state 4	NEW PRODUCTS future state 5
OPERATIONAL	Sales per Person	$7,472	$7,472	$8,493	$9,614	$7,472	$10,026
	On-Time Shipment	92%	94%	94%	94%	95%	94%
	First Time Through	71%	78%	78%	78%	78%	78%
	Dock-to-Dock Days	33.0	18.5	16.5	16.5	13.5	16.5
	Average Cost	$419.46	$413.97	$399.17	$366.14	$384.07	$366.14
	Accounts Receivable Days	54.0	50.0	50.0	50.0	50.0	50.0
CAPACITY Employee	Productive Capacity	51%	43%	64%	56%	43%	56%
	Non-Productive Capacity	30%	19%	27%	22%	19%	22%
	Available Capacity	19%	37%	9%	22%	37%	22%
CAPACITY Machines	Productive Capacity	53%	53%	59%	69%	53%	69%
	Non-Productive Capacity	32%	17%	19%	20%	17%	20%
	Available Capacity	15%	29%	22%	12%	29%	12%
FINANCIAL	Revenue	$332,569	$332,569	$332,569	$427,938	$332,569	$446,278
	Material Costs	$111,431	$108,446	$108,446	$139,545	$92,179	$139,545
	Conversion Costs	$116,753	$116,753	$108,704	$116,755	$116,755	$116,756
	Total Costs	$228,184	$225,199	$217,151	$256,300	$208,934	$256,301
	Value Stream Profit	$104,385	$107,370	$115,418	$171,638	$123,635	$189,977
	Return on Sales	31%	32%	35%	40%	37%	43%
	Inventory Value	$209,336	$113,026	$94,936	$118,113	$71,131	$118,114
	Cash Flow	$123,117	$288,926	$149,119	$185,283	$184,263	$203,622

Figure 48. Box score showing impact of planned value stream changes

Box Score #7 Quoting custom products	
Performance measures: • Productivity • Flow • Quality • Cost • Customer service • Stability	
Capacity • Productive • Nonproductive • Available	How much capacity is required to meet the demand of this quote?
Revenue	Price -- set by the customer based on value derived from product Volume -- what is the projected volume and time frame?
Material	Calculate the actual cost of material for this quote. If necessary, use Features and Characteristics to estimate material cost
Production Costs • Labor • Machines • Facilities • Other	To estimate the total production costs, use average cost per unit multiplied by a Features and Characteristics index. The Features and Characteristics index will use the quoted product's flow through the value stream
Value stream profit	Does the profitability of the order exceed minimum profitability requirements?

Box Score #8 Removing a product line or a customer	
Performance measures: • Productivity • Flow • Quality • Cost • Customer service • Stability	Calculate the future state of operational performance measures without the product line or customer demand
Capacity • Productive • Nonproductive • Available	Calculate the changes in capacity due to removing the product line or customer Is there demand to use any available capacity created?
Revenue	Calculate the revenue lost due to removing the product line or customer If demand exists, calculate total revenue
Material	Calculate the reduction in actual material cost due to removing the product line or customer Calculate the actual cost of material for any projected demand
Production Costs • Labor • Machines • Facilities • Other	Production costs do not decrease unless the available capacity created is transferred out of the value stream
Value stream profit	

For an example of this type of box score, see Figure 44.

D1: Planning and Budgeting

Background

Planning in a lean company is an integrated process. At its core, it embodies continuous application of the principles of organizational learning at every level of the company. These principles are shown in the "Plan, Do, Check, and Act" (PDCA) cycle. **See also section A1: c. for more information on PDCA.**

The PDCA process is a closed loop that establishes strategies and goals based upon an analysis of the current environment (PLAN), develops action programs to achieve the goals (DO), tests the effectiveness of the programs to achieve the goals (CHECK), updates operating policies and procedures for those programs that are effective (ACT). The consistent application of this method at every level of the business (i.e. company, value stream, cell/process) creates a continuous learning and change-oriented culture.

Having a structured process for planning fosters continuous organizational learning and enables the organization to change in pursuit of its strategic purpose, or vision. Effective planning cascades from vision to execution by using PDCA methodology to create change throughout the organization. The following diagram shows how this works.

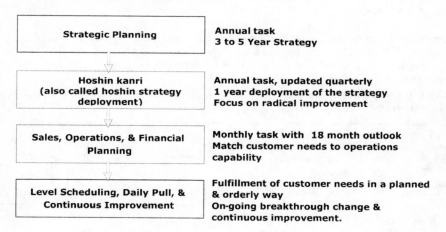

Figure 49. PDCA cascades from vision to execution

1. *Strategic planning: from vision to business strategy*—describing the products, services, customer groups and technologies by which the vision will be achieved
2. *Hoshin kanri / strategy deployment: from business strategy to value stream strategy*—linking the business goals to critical success factors, goals and action programs for each value stream of the business
3. *Sales operations and financial planning: from value stream strategy and customer demand to monthly value stream resource/improvement plans*—integrating sales, operations, product development and financial

resource planning with value stream resource/improvement plans
4. Level scheduling, daily management: from value stream resource plans to daily management—continuously adapting the business to meet the changing demands of customers and suppliers.

a. Hoshin strategy deployment

What is it?

Hoshin strategy deployment is a specific management process used to identify, communicate, manage and monitor improvement activities at all levels of the organization. It makes sure that the various activities that are happening within the company are correctly aligned with the company's strategy. Goals, actions, responsibilities, and measurements are included as essential components of the plan.

Hoshin strategy deployment ensures that strategies are implemented consistently throughout the organization. It makes sure that projects are aligned with approved strategic goals. This begins with a few high-level objectives that are critical to achieving the vision of the company.

Hoshin strategy deployment techniques can help achieve objectives when applied at any level:

1. Breakthrough objectives—involve new approaches to the business. An example would the new process structure depicted in a future state map.
2. Continuous improvement objectives—involve development of new methods within the existing framework.
3. Daily management objectives—involve getting done what has to be done daily within existing methods.

Link all measurements to improvement cycles. Motivate only lean behavior.

What does it do?

Hoshin strategy deployment provides an integrated way to apply the steps of the Plan, Do, Check, Act cycle.

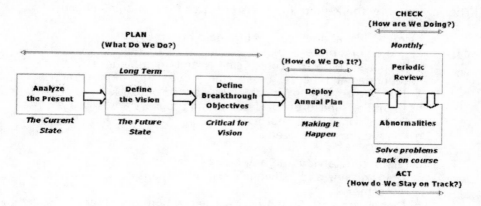

Figure 50. Putting PDCA to work

How do I do it?

At any level in the lean organization (corporate, plant, value stream and cell) the relationships between key factors are spelled out on what is termed an "X-matrix". The X-matrix chart includes the following elements:

1. Policies (strategies to achieve the higher level objectives.)
2. Objectives (critical success factors and projects required to achieve the strategies.)
3. Financial costs and benefits expected to result from the projects undertaken.
4. Measurement targets for the projects undertaken.
5. Who is responsible for getting the projects done.
6. When the projects are to be completed.

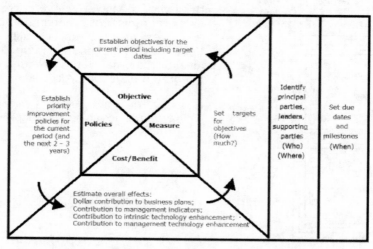

Figure 51. X-Matrix schematic; arrows indicate direction of rotation

77

The reasons why the X-matrix chart is effective for managing change:

1. It is simple, visual and actionable. The matrix:
   a. Fits on one piece of paper.
   b. Displays desired outcomes clearly and unambiguously.
   c. Identifies and focuses on specific activities for improvement.
   d. Identifies methods for achieving desired outcomes.
   e. Identifies measures for determining progress and success.
   f. Fosters continuous improvement.
   g. Clarifies resource needs.

2. It fosters accountability and buy-in. The matrix:
   a. Holds groups and individuals clearly responsible for specific outcomes.
   b. Clearly links every part of the organization to matrices that align improvement activities.
   c. Is initiated by management, but is co-created with input possible from every employee.

An entire set of hoshin strategy deployment X-matrix charts should be created to cascade strategy throughout the organization.

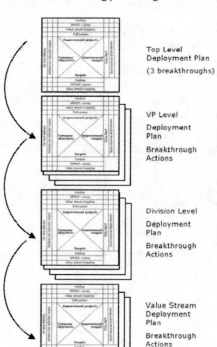

Top Level
Deployment Plan
(3 breakthroughs)

VP Level
Deployment
Plan

Breakthrough
Actions

Division Level
Deployment
Plan

Breakthrough
Actions

Value Stream
Deployment
Plan

Breakthrough
Actions

Here's how that would work:

After the top level matrix is created, the individuals and teams responsible for a particular set of objectives create their own charts. They do this by rotating the higher level matrix counter-clockwise, so that the higher-level "objective" now becomes the lower-level "policy." From this policy the lower level unit creates its own programs, costs/benefits, targets and measures, and responsibilities. Continue this procedure through every level of the organization creating a highly integrated planning process.

Figure 52. (left) Example of cascading methodology - hoshin strategy deployment

BMA Inc. The Lean Accounting Leaders

b. Sales operations and financial planning (SOFP)

Lean companies need a new way to do operations planning and budgeting — one that is integrated across functions and that is able to adapt to fluctuations in the business environment. We call this integrated planning and budgeting process "Sales, Operations and Financial Planning" (SOFP). Done properly, this integrated process will replace all operations, sales and other departmental planning, as well as budgeting.

What is it?

SOFP is standard work for planning. SOFP translates the sales forecast into the daily schedule of what will be built in the factory. Here are some of its attributes:

SOFP is a monthly process:
> It integrates sales planning, production planning, financial planning, new product planning, lean improvement plans and budgeting into a single, effective, cross-functional process.

Its inputs are:
> Eighteen-month functional plans for the value stream including:
>> Product family sales forecasts.
>> New product plans.
>> Production capacity plans.
>> Value stream costs.

Its outputs are:
> Integrated eighteen-month plans for the value stream including:
>> Sales plan—reflecting new product development and production capacity plan
>> New product development plan—reflecting sales plan and production capacity plan
>> Operations capacity plan, reflecting sales and new product development plans
>> Rolling eighteen month financial plan

The following diagram illustrates these relationships.

Figure 53. SOFP strategy integration

What does SOFP do?

SOFP aligns production capacity with sales demand in a structured way. This has both short term and longer term benefits, as follows:

Short term benefits	Longer term benefits
1. Establish production cycle times to match customer needs	1. Change staffing levels to meet future needs
2. Create level scheduling	2. Purchase or redeploy equipment
3. Recalculate kanbans	3. Make outsourcing decisions
4. Determine manpower levels for cells and the value stream	4. Adjust raw materials and component planning
5. Finalize project plans for new product introductions and continuous improvement activities	5. Develop new marketing strategies
6. Create month-end financial results in advance	6. Establish long-term continuous improvement plans
7. Initiate sales programs to make best use of resources	7. Structure budgeting and financial planning

In the short run, a lean company needs to have a good handle on the rate of production and the mix of products to be made each day to meet customer demand (takt).

This requires answers to the following questions:

1. What must the cycle time in the bottleneck operation be to fulfill customer takt?
2. What improvements have to be made to enable production to meet the takt of the anticipated demand?
3. Will the cell manpower levels need to be changed?
4. Will kanban sizes and quantities need to change?
5. What is the mix of products we expect to make to meet customer demand? How does this mix change?
6. How do we create level demand to maximize the flow through the value stream?
7. How does this change if we are a make to stock or a make to order company?

Very often the answers to these questions are not readily available but must be prepared in advance by having an accurate picture of future demand. With this picture in focus, operations management can create daily production plans that will enable efficient production of demanded items.

A longer term forecast of demand will enable the lean company to see what is coming over the horizon soon enough to react effectively. Resources can be put in place that will match capacity with demand. The lean company can also establish new product development and sales programs to fill capacity made available through lean improvements. Often the longer lead times for these initiatives require planning over the course of a year or more. Questions such as the following are important in this context:

1. Do we need to change manning levels to meet the needs of the customers—through cross training, adding new people, developing new skills?
2. Do we need to acquire or build equipment to meet future needs?
3. Are our existing suppliers able to provide the materials and components needed to meet future customer demand?
4. Will our existing sales and marketing programs be capable of filling the additional capacity freed up by lean improvements?
5. Will our new product plans fit with our lean plans and our long term sales forecast?

 SOFP creates a jointly agreed "game plan:" what we sell, what we make, and our cash flow.

Why use it?

Existing budgeting processes are inadequate to deal with the rapid changes in supply/demand relationships encountered by the twenty-first century manufacturer. Furthermore, there is often little or no coordination among plans developed in sales, operations, new product development and finance.

Some of the problems created by these out-of-sync plans are listed below:

1. Demand "shocks"
2. Lack of cooperative relationships throughout the value stream
3. Late deliveries caused by resource problems and material shortages
4. Invalid and out-of-date budgets driving wrong behaviors
5. Last minute capital investment requests, often poorly analyzed

What is needed is a way to continuously review the validity of planning assumptions, and update sales, operations and financial plans accordingly. The SOFP process fulfills this critical need.

How do I do it?

The SOFP process recurs monthly, on an eight-day cycle, as shown below:

Day 1-2	Day 3-4	Day 5	Day 6-7	Day 8
Value Stream Demand Planning	**Value Stream Operations Planning**	**SOFP Planning Meeting**	**Value Stream Financial Planning**	**Executive SOFP Meeting**
INPUT • Month-end data. • Customer forecasts • New product plans. OUTPUT • VS product family forecasts in units. • New SOFP Spreadsheet. WHO • Sales & marketing • New product development team	INPUT • Demand forecasts • Value stream cost analysis • Lean improvement plan • Value stream changes OUTPUT • VS capacity forecast • Updated SOFP sheets WHO • Production operations	INPUT • SOFP spreadsheet OUTPUT • Decisions to balance demand & capacity • VS improvement plan • New product introduction plan • Month-end financials • Agenda for Executive SOFP Meeting WHO • Value stream mgrs • Sales & marketing • New product develop • VS Finance • Other key operations people	INPUT • SOFP spreadsheet OUTPUT • Updated rolling budgets for next 18 months • Major budget issues list • Major new expenditure WHO • VS Finance • Plant or Division controller	INPUT • SOFP spreadsheets • Executive SOFP Meeting agenda • Updated budgets • Major budget issues • Major new expenditure OUTPUT • Operational decisions • Authorized business "game plan" • Financial decisions WHO • President • Senior managers • Value stream mgrs • Sales & marketing • New products • Other key people

Figure 54. SOFP cycle

Days 1-2: Value Stream Demand Planning

The starting point for SOFP is a clear definition of the value streams and of the product families that flow through them. This provides the basis for the eighteen- month rolling forecast. With that as a foundation, you can proceed to set up the forecast.

Some principles of the forecast:

1. Sales and marketing own the forecasts. They are accountable as part of the SOFP team for the development, authorization and execution of the demand forecasts.
2. The forecast should be at the value stream or product family level— whichever is more meaningful—but not at the product level.
3. Always forecast units, not dollars—that will come later.
4. Don't argue about forecast accuracy; improve the process and make it better.
5. Always record and report any assumptions underlying the forecasts.
6. Always measure forecast error and forecast bias.

The output of the forecasting process should look something like the schedule below:

VALUE STREAM: OEM Products														
	HISTORY													
SALES	Apr-07	May-07	Jun-07	Jul-07	Aug-07	Sep-07	Oct-07	Nov-07	Dec-07	Qtr-1-08	Qtr-2-08	Qtr-3-08	Qtr-4-08
New Forecast	1950	2415	2300	2700	2432	2352	2662	3201	1869	7524	7576	7632	7712
Actual Sales	1968	2440	2176	0	0	0	0	0	0	0	0	0	0
Difference: Month	1668	25	-124	0	0	0	0	0	0	0	0	0	0
Difference: Cum	1668	1693	1569										

Figure 55. SOFP spreadsheet - demand

Questions to consider:

1. What is the right unit of measure for the monthly forecast?
2. Where will the forecast data come from?
3. What forecasting methods are appropriate?
4. Can you get accurate forecasts from major customers?
5. How will you get valid forecasts for new product introductions?
6. How will forecast assumptions be documented and reviewed?
7. Can you create a continuous improvement process for forecasting?
8. Will sales and marketing assume responsibility for forecasting and its outcomes?

Days 3-4: Value Stream Operations Planning

The completed demand forecast becomes the input to the operations plan.

The primary concern here is whether operations have the capacity to meet forecasted customer demand. Capacity is constrained by how many units flow through the bottleneck operation, any obstacles to flow through the entire value stream (such as scrap, rework, downtime, wait-time), and any endemic production problems such as materials shortages, absenteeism and the like. Changes in operations have the ability to change the production capacity over time—changes such as:

1. Improvements in the bottleneck process or eliminating the bottleneck

altogether.
2. Kaizen events at the bottleneck.
3. Adding new equipment or more people.
4. Improved processes, such as through elimination of scrap, rework, machine downtime.
5. Standardization of the work.
6. Changes in product mix.

The operations planning process should consider the effects of these changes on their ability to meet planned demand.

The output from this step should look something like the schedule below:

VALUE STREAM: OEM Products

SALES	HISTORY			Jul-07	Aug-07	Sep-07	Oct-07	Nov-07	Dec-07	Qtr-1-08	Qtr-2-08	Qtr-3-08	Qtr-4-08
	Apr-07	May-07	Jun-07										
New Forecast	1950	2415	2300	2700	2432	2352	2662	3201	1869	7524	7576	7632	7712
Actual Sales	1968	2440	2176	0	0	0	0	0	0	0	0	0	0
Difference: Month	1668	25	-124	0	0	0	0	0	0	0	0	0	0
Difference: Cum	1668	1693	1569										
OPERATIONS													
Old Plan	2400	2520	2286	2640	2291	2857	2112	2291	1714	5142	5142	5142	5142
New Plan	2400	2520	2286	2640	0	0							
New vs Old			0		-2291	-2857	-2112	-2291	-1714	-5142	-5142	-5142	-5142
Calculated Plan				2640	2520	3000	2904	3120	2316	7536	7589	7650	7712
Actual	2080	2140	2248										
Difference: Month	-320	-380	-38										
Difference: Cum	-320	-700	-738										
Max Capacity	2880	2520	2400	2640	2520	3000	2904	3120	2529	8040	8040	8040	8040
Days in Period	20	21	20	22	21	25	22	21	15	67	67	67	67
Takt Time Sec	535	454	454	425	451	555	431	342	419	465	462	458	454
Cycle Time Sec	363	435	435	435	435	435	395	351	310	435	435	435	435
Cycle/Takt Ratio	68%	96%	96%	102%	97%	78%	92%	103%	74%	94%	94%	95%	96%
Bottleneck Capacity	-22%	-25%	-19%	-25%	-25%	-27%	-15%	-42%	-3%	4%	4%	4%	4%

Figure 56. SOFP spreadsheet - forecast and operations

Day 5: Balancing Demand and Capacity

The purpose of this meeting is to create a plan for actions needed to balance capacity to the planned demand. These include consideration of both the short term and longer term actions reviewed earlier in this chapter.
The input to this meeting is the SOFP spreadsheet like the one in Figure 57.

VALUE STREAM: OEM Products

SALES	HISTORY			Jul-07	Aug-07	Sep-07	Oct-07	Nov-07	Dec-07	Qtr-1-08	Qtr-2-08	Qtr-3-08	Qtr-4-08
	Apr-07	May-07	Jun-07										
New Forecast	1950	2415	2300	2700	2432	2352	2662	3201	1869	7524	7576	7632	7712
Actual Sales	1968	2440	2176	0	0	0	0	0	0	0	0	0	0
Difference: Month	1668	25	-124	0	0	0	0	0	0	0	0	0	0
Difference: Cum	1668	1693	1569										
OPERATIONS													
Old Plan	2400	2520	2286	2640	2291	2857	2112	2291	1714	5142	5142	5142	5142
New Plan	2400	2520	2286	2640	0	0							
New vs Old			0		-2291	-2857	-2112	-2291	-1714	-5142	-5142	-5142	-5142
Calculated Plan				2640	2520	3000	2904	3120	2316	7536	7589	7650	7712
Actual	2080	2140	2248										
Difference: Month	-320	-380	-38										
Difference: Cum	-320	-700	-738										
Max Capacity	2880	2520	2400	2640	2520	3000	2904	3120	2529	8040	8040	8040	8040
Days in Period	20	21	20	22	21	25	22	21	15	67	67	67	67
Takt Time Sec	535	454	454	425	451	555	431	342	419	465	462	458	454
Cycle Time Sec	363	435	435	435	435	435	395	351	310	435	435	435	435
Cycle/Takt Ratio	68%	96%	96%	102%	97%	78%	92%	103%	74%	94%	94%	95%	96%
Bottleneck Capacity	-22%	-25%	-19%	-25%	-25%	-27%	-15%	-42%	-3%	4%	4%	4%	4%
INVENTORY													
Inventory Qty	1255	1233	400	340	428	1076	1318	1237	1684	1696	1709	1727	1727
Days	10.91	10.72	3.26	2.94	4.55	8.89	8.65	9.93	15.00	15.00	15.00	15.00	15.00
Planned Inventory Days													
RM	18.60	12.33	7.70	3.50	3.50	2.76	3.38	2.01	1.75	5.00	5.00	5.00	5.00
WIP	7.20	7.10	5.30	4.90	4.20	4.34	4.22	2.20	3.35	2.00	2.00	2.00	2.00
FG	10.91	10.72	3.26	15.00	15.00	15.00	15.00	15.00	15.00	15.00	15.00	15.00	15.00
TOTAL	36.71	30.15	16.26	23.40	22.70	22.10	22.60	19.21	20.10	22.00	22.00	22.00	22.00

Figure 57. SOFP spreadsheet - forecast, operations, and inventory (supply)

The outputs of the SOFP meeting include the following:

1. An integrated plan for each value stream for sales, operations, new product introduction, and continuous improvement.
2. A set of solutions to the problems of balancing demand and capacity—both short and long term.
3. Documentation of any assumptions that underlie the plan.
4. An agenda for the executive SOFP meeting and recommendations for action.

Days 6-7: Value Stream Financial Planning and Budgeting

The operations forecast, once signed off, can easily be converted to a financial forecast for the value stream.

This is very important in a lean company, because the traditional annual budgeting process lacks capability to provide a financial roadmap for the lean value stream, for the following reasons:

1. It takes too long to put together. The annual budget in most companies consumes total management time between September and December of each year.
2. It is out of date when it goes into effect on January 1. A budget is only as good as the forecast assumptions that go into it. For most companies these assumptions change rapidly, often monthly or even more frequently. A budget prepared before the start of the year for which it is intended can not be expected to be valid throughout the year.
3. It is inflexible. Often companies will not change the budget which consumed so many resources to prepare.
4. It is politically driven. The budget is used as a performance "contract" with management. There are often penalties for missing budget targets. This often causes managers to understate their financial and operating goals for the year, resulting in performance projections that are artificially low, and possibly lower than necessary to meet competitive threats and take advantage of opportunities. A severe distortion is injected into the planning process.

SOFP is well suited to replace the annual budgeting process for the following reasons:

1. It creates budgets and financial plans every month using the most recent and best data.
2. The team uses the same data for financial and operational planning.
3. The budgets are updated every month.
4. The budgets roll 12, 15, or 18 months into the future.
5. The budgets are always up-to-date and actionable.
6. The budgets are realistic about the long-term picture.

An example of the financial forecast is shown in Figure 58. This forecast is a direct outcome of the sales and operations forecasts worked out through the SOFP process described above. It is prepared at a summary level and should be accompanied with more detailed breakdowns, assumptions and explanations of budgeted numbers.

VALUE STREAM: OEM Products												
	HISTORY											
SALES	Apr-07	May-07	Jun-07	Jul-07	Aug-07	Sep-07	Oct-07	Nov-07	Dec-07	Qtr-1-08	Qtr-2-08	Qtr-3-08	Qtr-4-08
New Forecast	1950	2415	2300	2700	2432	2352	2962	3201	1889	7524	7576	7632	7712
Actual Sales	1968	2440	2176	0	0	0	0	0	0	0	0	0	0
Difference: Month	1668	25	-124	0	0	0	0	0	0	0	0	0	0
Difference: Cum	1668	1693	1569										
OPERATIONS													
Old Plan	2400	2520	2286	2640	2291	2657	2112	2291	1714	5142	5142	5142	5142
New Plan	2400	2520	2286	2640	0								
New vs Old				0	-2291	-2857	-2112	-2291	-1714	-5142	-5142	-5142	-5142
Calculated Plan				2640	2520	3000	2904	3120	2316	7536	7589	7650	7712
Actual	2080	2140	2248										
Difference: Month	-320	-360	-38										
Difference: Cum	-320	-700	-738										
Max Capacity	2880	2520	2400	2640	2520	3000	2904	3120	2529	8040	8040	8040	8040
Days in Period	20	21	20	22	21	25	22	21	15	67	67	67	67
Takt Time Sec	535	454	454	425	451	555	431	342	419	465	462	458	454
Cycle Time Sec	363	435	435	435	435	435	395	351	310	435	435	435	435
Cycle/Takt Ratio	68%	96%	96%	102%	97%	78%	92%	103%	74%	94%	94%	95%	96%
Bottleneck Capacity	-22%	-25%	-19%	-25%	-25%	-27%	-15%	-42%	-3%	4%	4%	4%	4%
INVENTORY													
Inventory Qty	1255	1233	400	340	428	1076	1318	1237	1684	1696	1709	1727	1727
Days	10.91	10.72	3.26	2.94	4.55	8.89	8.65	9.93	15.00	15.00	15.00	15.00	15.00
Planned Inventory Days													
RM	18.60	12.33	7.70	3.50	3.50	2.76	3.38	2.01	1.75	5.00	5.00	5.00	5.00
WIP	7.20	7.10	5.30	4.90	4.20	4.34	4.22	2.20	3.35	2.00	2.00	2.00	2.00
FG	10.91	10.72	3.26	15.00	15.00	15.00	15.00	15.00	15.00	15.00	15.00	15.00	15.00
TOTAL	36.71	30.15	16.26	23.40	22.70	22.10	22.60	19.21	20.10	22.00	22.00	22.00	22.00
FINANCIAL													
Revenue	$710,586	$903,788	$801,946	$995,062	$896,293	$866,809	$981,057	$1,179,701	$688,804	$2,772,905	$2,792,069	$2,812,708	$2,842,191
Material	$240,073	$310,520	$276,245	$490,039	$346,660	$348,721	$431,184	$411,659	$283,653	$1,199,813	$1,140,025	$1,179,945	$1,194,113
Conversion	$305,053	$330,683	$310,019	$341,164	$327,356	$388,309	$341,915	$326,606	$233,124	$1,041,556	$1,041,613	$1,041,554	$1,041,574
Profit	$165,461	$262,386	$215,682	$163,859	$222,277	$129,779	$207,958	$441,436	$172,026	$531,536	$610,431	$591,208	$606,504
ROS	23.29%	29.03%	26.89%	16.47%	24.80%	14.97%	21.20%	37.42%	24.97%	19.17%	21.86%	21.02%	21.34%
Inventory	$434,191	$344,544	$238,412	$168,306	$151,271	$145,049	$149,559	$81,863	$106,532	$116,026	$118,058	$118,120	$118,071

Figure 58. SOFP spreadsheet - including financial information

The forecast is prepared by value stream. The components of this forecast are straightforward.

1. Revenue is derived from the sales forecast in units and by a forecast of prices expected to be charged.
2. Material costs are raw materials, components and outside processing used to manufacture the products forecasted, assuming that the items are purchased for the value stream and expensed upon receipt.
3. Conversion costs are the period costs of the resources assigned to the value stream, as follows:
   a. Employee wages and benefits
   b. Machine depreciation
   c. Facilities costs including lease, utilities, maintenance and the like—based on the square feet occupied by the value stream
   d. Other required costs such as tooling, supplies, MRO costs and administration.
4. Any new capital expenditures required.

The financial forecast is included with the package prepared for the Executive SOFP meeting. This ensures that when the SOFP plan is approved, the budget is also approved.

Day 8: SOFP Executive Meeting

The purposes of the SOFP executive meeting are:

1. To make decisions for each value stream, either accepting the recommendations from the SOFP meeting or choosing a different path.
2. To authorize changes to production rates.
3. To resolve issues that could not be agreed at the SOFP meeting.
4. To authorize improvement and new product plans.
5. To authorize the new budget.

A typical agenda would include the following:

1. Macro review of the business.
2. Review current value stream box scores.
3. Review new product introduction plans.
4. Review each value stream spreadsheet and decisions, namely:
   a. Forecasts
   b. Takt time and cycle time
   c. Significant short-term changes
   d. Significant long-term changes
5. Review financial information
   a. Month-end P&L
   b. New budgets
   c. Major financial changes
6. Recap and document decisions made
7. Critique the effectiveness of the meeting

Keys to a successful Executive SOFP meeting include:

1. Keep the meeting short—less than 90 minutes
2. President of the unit must be the chairperson
3. Spreadsheets and decision lists must be complete, accurate and understandable
4. Stick to the point of the meeting

Remember SOFP is quite simple, but it is difficult to implement because it represents a substantial change in the way most companies do business. Expect that it will take at least six months before the process is perfected. Be patient!

SOFP eliminates lots of waste, for instance:- last minute chaotic crisis management- the need for complex production planning and shop-floor control systems and departments- expediting because production rates are pre-planned- hosts of formal and informal planning meetings

D2: The Financial Impact of Lean Improvement

Why use it?

Calculating the financial benefits of lean is an important part of a lean business strategy. It forces company management to begin addressing the success of a lean implementation before the success occurs.

Finance has a crucial role to play. They can lead a cross functional effort to understand what is happening financially as a result of lean manufacturing. And they can address how the company will make use of the productive capacity that is freed up as lean manufacturing matures.

Many lean manufacturing efforts flounder because company managers do not clearly understand the true financial impacts of the lean improvements they are making.

A lean business strategy is a business growth strategy. How this strategy works can be best summarized as follows: lean principles, practices, tools and methods are used effectively to create a culture of continuous improvement, which reduces and eliminates wasteful activities and inventory and creates available productive capacity.

Lean companies make money by increasing sales to make use of that productive capacity and by developing other sound business improvements to reallocate and eliminate unused resources.

What does it do?

The financial analysis required to show the impact of lean manufacturing must take into consideration the changes in the company's production capacity due to continuous improvement.

The traditional company income statement simply shows how money was spent, not how well it was spent. It also does not show the cost of available capacity. Traditional analyses using standard costing do not clearly explain the financial impacts of lean. In fact, many times financial analyses of lean using standard costing may conclude lean is not working to boost the company's bottom line, when in fact good lean things are happening every day.

How do I do it?

a. Value stream mapping

The first step in this process is to understand the "future state" of a lean implementation, as embodied in the value stream map. Lean manufacturing uses current state and future state value stream maps to plan continuous improvements. After the current state map is created, a lean implementation team will create a future state map that identifies what wasteful activities will be eliminated and how much productive capacity will be created as a result of lean change. Future state maps are usually created for 6-12 months after lean implementation begins. Some lean implementations also create a longer-term future state map for 2-3 years out.

b. Value stream capacity analysis

After you create the value stream maps, an analysis of value stream capacity must be completed. The data boxes from both the current state and future state value stream maps provide the information needed to calculate:

1. Productive or value-added capacity
2. Non-productive or non-value added capacity
3. Available capacity

The capacity for each process step in the value stream is calculated using the following steps:

Step 1. Calculate the Total Available Employee Time
   (#employees x #days x Labor Hrs per shift)
Step 2. Calculate the Employee Productive Time
   (Qty per Month x Cycle Time x Crew Size)
Step 3. Calculate the Employee Productive Capacity Percentage.
   (Employee Productive Time / Total Available Time)
Step 4. Calculate change-over time, scrap and rework time, downtime, inspection time.
   C/O = (quantity/batch size) x Change-over time
   Scrap/rework = Qty x (scrap + rework rate) x Cycle Time
   D/T = Downtime% x Total Available Time
   Inspection= (Inspect% x Quantity) x Inspection time
Step 5. Calculate the Total Non-Productive Time
   Step 4 plus 5S and meetings
Step 6. Calculate the Employee Non-Productive Capacity Percentage
   Total Non-Prod Time / Total Available Time
Step 7. Calculate the Employee Available Capacity Percentage.
   100% - (Prod. Capacity + Non-Prod Capacity)

This is easier to visualize with an example. The chart on the next page shows the current and future state capacity for a process in a typical value stream.

In this example, the company is planning to make improvements in the following areas:

Reduce change over time by 75%
Reduce batch size
Improve scrap rate by 20%
Improve rework by 50%
Eliminate downtime
Eliminate inspection

Making these changes will result in a radical reduction of non-productive capacity coupled with an increase in available capacity without any change in employee productive capacity.

	Current State	Kaizen Improvement	Future State 1
Employee Productive Capacity	44%		44%
Employee Non-Productive Capacity	43%		17%
Employee Available Capacity	13%		38%
Quantity per Month	10000		10000
Employee Cycle Time	120		120
Internal Change Over Time Sec	10800	75% improvement	2700
External Change-Over Sec	0		0
Labor Hours per shift	7.50		7.50
# Shifts per day	1		1
Average Batch Size	500	Reduce to 300	300
Scrap Rate	20%	20% improvement	16%
Rework Rate	20%	50% improvement	10%
Downtime %	10%	Eliminated	0%
Inspection %	10%	Eliminated	0%
Inspection Time Sec	120		120
Crew Size	1		1
# cells	2		2
Number of Employees	5		5
Days per month	20		20
Total Available Employee Time	2,700,000		2,700,000
Productive Time	1,200,000		1,200,000
Change Over Time Sec	216,000		90,000
Scrap & Rework Time	480,000		312,000
Downtime	270,000		0
Inspection Time	120,000		0
5S & Clean up	60,000		60,000
Meetings & reporting	6,000		6,000
Improvement projects	0		0
Total Non-Productive Time	1,152,000		468,000

Figure 59. Value stream capacity analysis example

BMA Inc. The Lean Accounting Leaders

This first phase of kaizen improvements begs the question: "What should the company do with the capacity that has been made available?"

Eliminating waste and freeing up capacity is like finding hidden treasure on the factory floor!

Using this type of analysis, a cross-functional team can figure out how to use freed up capacity to grow revenue. They can also look at capacity management alternatives for using or eliminating excess capacity.

Revenue growth opportunities should be looked at in the classic marketing approach:

Can we sell more existing products to existing customers?
Can we develop new customers for our existing products?
Can we develop new products for existing customers?
Can we develop new products for new customers?

Here are some issues to consider when reviewing options for revenue generation:

1. What impact will lead time reduction have on your competitive position in existing markets?
2. How can you position yourself against your competitors if your lead times are less that theirs?
3. If lean principles are applied to the product development process, what impact will this have on generating revenue from new products?
4. How much available capacity will be used in generating this revenue?

In the area of capacity management, the focus should be on reallocating existing capacity and exploring alternatives for divesting excess capacity.

Reallocating capacity -- issues to consider:

1. Can we cross train employees to create a more flexible workforce? A cross training program should be part of continuous improvement; its progress should be tracked by performance measurements.
2. Can we assign available employees to continuous improvement activities when productive activities are not available? A formal company-wide continuous improvement program should be created that identifies employees with available capacity and matches them to continuous improvement activities.
3. Can we bring outsourced activities in-house? All outsourced production activities should be analyzed to determine if the company possesses the resources to perform these activities in-house by making use of available capacity. If the resources exist, bringing outsourced

activities in house will reduce costs.

4. Can we become a contract manufacturer? If your company possesses a particular core manufacturing process competency, explore the possibility of using that competency to produce products outside of your normal product families.

Strategies for divesting excess capacity:

1. Develop an employee attrition program, where full-time employees who leave the company are not replaced. A sound cross-training program makes an attrition program possible.
2. Reduce or eliminate overtime.
3. Freeze full-time hiring and begin a temporary workforce program. This program requires the company to create a pool of temporary workers that can be called on to meet spikes in customer demand, and who don't work if not needed. Additionally, a temporary worker program identifies potential full-time employees with the specific skills and experience that could be needed if a full-time employee must be replaced, or if demand increases sufficiently to warrant hiring full-time employees.
4. Sell excess machinery and equipment.
5. Reduce your facility size or rent excess space.

Each alternative should be analyzed using lean decision-making techniques and in conformity with lean principles.

c. Box scores with plans for financial benefits

The box score should be the primary analysis tool when evaluating the financial benefits of lean. Why? The box score will accurately illustrate how business decisions that have positive impact on operational and capacity improvement will yield future financial improvement.

See also section B.1.c. for more details about constructing box scores.

The output of reviewing alternatives should be a comprehensive plan to present to senior executives with a financial analysis of each alternative and an explanation of each alternative's impact on the overall financial position of the company. This plan should be based on lean accounting principles, practices and tools.

It is important for this plan to be presented to senior management as soon as possible after a future state value stream map has been created, because it may take considerable time to implement some of the alternatives discussed above. The foundations for new programs, policies and initiatives need to be in place so they can be implemented quickly as capacity becomes available.

One of the roles of finance, and its leadership, in any organization is to be an objective, non-partisan advisor to executives as to the financial soundness of business decisions. Many, but not all, lean initiatives begin at the operational level and at some point need executive approval. By leading the effort to show the financial benefits of lean, and by using lean accounting methods, the finance team will clearly show executives that the transformation to a lean company will achieve positive financial results.

		Current State - Before Lean	Future State Lean Step One	Future State Lean Step Two	Future State Longer Term
		Dec-02	Jan-Jun 2003	Jul-Dec 2003	Jan-Jun 2004
OPERATIONAL	Sales per Person	$224,833	$224,833	$224,833	$277,031
	Inventory Turns	6.5	10	15	20
	Average Cost per Unit	$31.32	$31.32	29.88	24.25
	First Time Through	81.00%	95.00%	90.00%	95.00%
	Lead Time in Days	25.00	5.00	5.00	2.50
CAPACITY	Productive	55%	52%	52%	79%
	Non-Productive	42%	40%	12%	12%
	Available Capacity	3%	8%	36%	9%
FINANCIAL	Revenue	$4,062,000	$4,062,000	$4,062,000	$5,686,000
	Material Costs	$1,164,184	$1,164,184	$1,109,327.16	$1,552,839.55
	Conversion Costs	$1,483,416	$1,483,416	$1,483,416	$1,657,500
	Value Stream Profit	$1,414,400	$1,414,400	$1,469,257	$2,475,660
	Value Stream ROS	34.82%	34.82%	36.17%	43.54%
40.00%	Hurdle Rate	-5.18%	-5.18%	-3.83%	3.54%

Figure 60. Example of box score showing impacts of lean changes

D3. Lean Capital Planning

Why use it?

The capital planning process in a lean organization is related to capacity management. Lean companies strive for flexible, just-in-time capacity to meet current and usually level demand, rather than adding (or subtracting) large amounts of capacity to meet changing situations.

This lean approach to capacity management requires a different analysis model than the traditional discounted cash flow or return on investment analyses.

What does it do?

Capital planning from a lean perspective creates a disciplined process of analyzing and solving capacity issues and links capital planning to the SOFP process. See also Section D.1.b. about SOFP

A lean capital planning process examines many alternatives to solve capacity issues.   This approach assesses the impact of continuous improvement on capacity, before purchasing equipment. It also ensures that investments are spent on appropriate equipment rather than on purchasing large pieces of equipment that create large amounts of excess capacity.

How do I do it?

Lean capital planning starts at the strategic level. As part of the strategic planning process, a company identifies key projects or initiatives that are required to meet strategic objectives. Senior management identifies the resources required for these strategic initiatives, which often include capital equipment requirements. These capital equipment requirements serve as an estimate, which will be used throughout the organization for detailed planning.

The actual planning for capital purchases occurs at the value stream level, usually as part of the SOFP process. One of the primary outcomes of the monthly SOFP process is identifying the need for changes in capacity over the long term.

Because lean companies are careful with capital investment, they go through a thorough investigation of multiple solutions to the problem -- ensuring there is enough capacity to meet long-term demand -- before committing to a particular course of action.

We use a six-step process for evaluating capital purchases.

Step 1: Use the value stream box score capacity analysis to assess the impact of capital equipment plans. To calculate capacity the following information is needed:

1. Current state value stream map.
2. Future state value stream map.
3. Value stream capacity analysis.
4. Current demand and demand trends.

The data from the current state and future state value stream maps is input into the value stream capacity analysis spreadsheet (an example is shown below in Figure 61 next page) which calculates the productive, non-productive and available capacity of the value stream. Comparing current and future state value stream maps tells the value stream manager how much capacity will be created due to continuous improvement.

See also section B.2.a. about value stream costing.

CELL NUMBER	Fine Blank	Tumble Deburr	Double Disk	Stamp	Nail Notch	Water Wash
Employee Productive Capacity	0%	0%	29%	68%	58%	
Employee Non-Productive Capacity	68%	59%	54%	18%	19%	
Employee Available Capacity	32%	41%	17%	15%	23%	
Quantity per Month	108,000	108,000	108,000	54,000	45,958	108,000
Employee Cycle Time	0	0	3	7	7	0
Internal Change Over Time Sec	900	900	1800	600	1200	120
External Change-Over Sec	1800	0	10800	0	0	0
Labor Hours per shift	9.67	9.67	9.67	9.67	9.67	9.67
# Shifts per day	2	2	2	2	2	2
Average Batch Size	3000	3000	3000	3000	3000	1000
Scrap Rate	12.0%	11.0%	8.0%	0.1%	0.0%	0.0%
Rework Rate	4.0%	5.0%	3.0%	0.0%	0.0%	0.0%
Downtime %	11.0%	9.0%	5.0%	0.0%	0.6%	0.0%
Inspection %	12.0%	10.0%	10.0%	0.0%	0.0%	0.0%
Inspection Time Sec	15	15	25	0	0	
Crew Size	1	1	1	1	1	1
# cells	2	1	3	1	2	1
Number of Employees	1	1	2	1	1	0
Days per month	16	16	16	16	16	16
Total Available Employee Time	556,800	556,800	1,113,600	556,800	556,800	0
Productive Time	0	0	324,000	378,000	321,706	0
Change Over Time Sec	97,200	32,400	64,800	10,800	18,383	12,960
Scrap & Rework Time	0	0	35,640	504	0	0
Downtime	0	50,112	55,680	0	3,480	0
Inspection Time	194,400	162,000	270,000	0	0	0
5S & Clean up	57,600	57,600	115,200	57,600	57,600	0
Meetings & reporting	28,800	28,800	57,600	28,800	28,800	0
Improvement projects	0	0	0	0	0	0
Total Non-Productive Time	378,000	330,912	598,920	97,704	108,263	12,960

Figure 61. Value stream capacity analysis for capital planning

Step 2: Develop a long-term demand forecast. This is typically part of the SOFP process, but if SOFP has not matured, the value stream manager would work with sales and marketing to develop the forecast.

Step 3: Use the value stream capacity analysis to project the forecast's impact on capacity (see Figure 61). In our example, a 20% increase in sales reduces available capacity to 9%.

	Current State	Kaizen Improvement	Future State 1	Business Decisions	Future State 2	Business Decisions	Future State 3
Employee Productive Capacity	44%		44%		67%		87%
Employee Non-Productive Capacity	43%		17%		25%		18%
Employee Available Capacity	13%		38%		9%		-4%
Quantity per Month	10000		10000	Increase Sales 20%	12000	Increase 30%	15600
Employee Cycle Time	120		120		130		120
Internal Change Over Time Sec	10800	75% improvement	2700		2700		2700
External Change-Over Sec	0		0		0		0
Labor Hours per shift	7.50		7.50		7.50		7.50
# Shifts per day	1		1		1		1
Average Batch Size	500	Reduce to 300	300		300		300
Scrap Rate	20%	20% improvement	16%		16%	Improved Std.Work	5%
Rework Rate	20%	50% improvement	10%		10%		5%
Downtime %	10%	Eliminated	0%		0%		0%
Inspection %	10%	Eliminated	0%		0%		0%
Inspection Time Sec	120		120		120		120
Crew Size	1		1		1		1
# cells	2		2		2		2
Number of Employees	5		5	Redeploy 1 person	4		4
Days per month	20		20		20		20
Total Available Employee Time	2,700,000		2,700,000		2,160,000		2,160,000
Productive Time	1,200,000		1,200,000		1,440,000		1,872,000
Change Over Time Sec	216,000		90,000		108,000		140,400
Scrap & Rework Time	480,000		312,000		374,400		187,200
Downtime	270,000		0		0		0
Inspection Time	120,000		0		0		0
SS & Clean up	60,000		60,000		48,000		48,000
Meetings & reporting	6,000		6,000		6,000		6,000
Improvement projects	0		0		0		0
Total Non-Productive Time	1,152,000		468,000		536,400		381,600

Figure 62. Value stream capital planning example

Continuing with the analysis in Figure 61, the company might then determine that 9% available capacity (in future state 2) is not enough, given the forecasted 20% increase in demand. Senior management and value stream management would then assess the choices in purchasing capital equipment.

Step 4. Determine whether new equipment is necessary.

In lean companies it is usually preferable to purchase smaller rather than larger pieces of equipment. Large equipment is more expensive and provides large amounts of capacity, beyond what the company might need to meet projected demand. This is wasteful and counter to lean principles. In addition it is unlikely that the company can accurately forecast the 3 or 5 year projections required for traditional DCF or ROI approaches.

Additionally, lean value streams use other methods to determine the best solution for equipment purchase decisions. Because the solution has to conform with the principles of lean, managers would questions like: Does the solution support or improve continuous flow? Does it inherent mistake-

BMA Inc. The Lean Accounting Leaders

proofing? Is it safe, easy to train and use? Does it fit with takt time? Will there be too much capacity? If so, what is it used for? Are we adding the equipment for a value adding process, and the like. Many of these types of considerations are listed in the table below.

Meet takt time	No tool room maintenance
One piece flow	Tooling cost
Operator involvement	As simple as possible
Hanedashi (self unload)	Readily available equipment
Chaku-Chaku (load)	6 Sigma process capability
Poke-Yoke (mistake proof)	Known process
Minimal capital	Maintenance machines
Incremental capacity	Familiar technology
100% gauging	Flexible machines
Value added operation	Jidoka (autonomation)
SMED change over	Minimal time to develop
3D (dangerous, dirty, difficult)	

Figure 63. Considerations for capital purchases

Step 5: Analyze the financial impact of the equipment purchase decision using the value stream P&L. Adding equipment will increase machine costs in the value stream by the amount of annual depreciation and any other specific expenses which can be identified. Offsetting revenue and margin may also increase if the additional capacity will allow the company to meet demand.

Step 6: Construct a box score based on your analysis that shows when additional capital should be purchased. In the following example (Figure 63), the company is introducing a new product family into a value stream. The demand forecast is projected for 36 months from 1 unit per month to 30 per month. Based on this demand, the value stream is able to project the impact on capacity. The box score shows that when demand reaches 5 units per month, it will be time to invest in additional machines (and people) to increase available capacity from 7 % to 31%. This investment in machines and people will increase conversion costs by $23,000 per month, but profit will also increase $33,643 per month, because the value stream will have the capacity to meet double the demand.

	Current	6 Months	1 Year	18 Months	2 Years	30 Months	3 Years
Additional Monthly Quantity	0	1	5	10	15	20	30
OPERATIONAL							
Units per Person	1.52	1.54	1.63	1.80	1.90	2.16	2.59
On-Time Shipment	100%	100%	100%	100%	100%	100%	100%
Dock-to-Dock Days	6.00	6.00	6.00	5.00	5.00	4.50	4.50
First Time Through	80%	80%	85%	85%	85%	85%	85%
Average Product Cost	$3,481	$3,490	$3,278	$2,965	$2,821	$2,497	$2,092
AR Days	42	42	42	42	37	37	37
CAPACITY							
Productive	29%	33%	38%	34%	36%	41%	50%
Non-Productive	54%	52%	55%	35%	33%	33%	33%
Available Capacity	17%	15%	7%	31%	31%	26%	17%
FINANCIAL							
Revenue	$466,670	$472,670	$502,568	$562,461	$630,170	$714,132	$834,172
Material Costs	$172,085	$175,385	$178,695	$181,935	$184,686	$187,101	$189,160
Conversion Costs	$119,584	$119,584	$119,584	$142,584	$142,584	$152,593	$158,084
Value Stream Gross Profit	$175,001	$177,701	$204,299	$237,942	$302,900	$374,438	$486,928
Value Stream ROS	37.50%	37.60%	40.65%	42.30%	48.07%	52.43%	58.37%
Additional People				5		2	1
Additional Machines				3		2	1
Material Costs per Unit		$3,300	$3,300	$3,250	$2,750	$2,325	$2,150

Figure 64.   Box score analysis for capital planning

Exclusively using traditional capital acquisition analysis tools such as discounted cash flow and return on investment usually lead to the decision to purchase large, specialized equipment.   This equipment often becomes a monument in the production process. By using box score analysis in the capital planning process, a lean company can assess the viability of a capital purchase on operations and capacity and ensure that it makes financial sense.

BMA Inc. The Lean Accounting Leaders

D4. Invest In People

Background

Management in a lean company involves not only managing the value stream, but also managing the value stream team.

The culture of continuous improvement that is at the heart of lean requires an environment of mutual trust among employees that leads to individual creativity and teamwork.

Merely installing the methods of lean without investing in the people who will make it happen will ensure that the benefits achieved will be limited and short-lived.

From the perspective of lean accounting the role of the manager in a lean company must change: from managing by results to managing the process to achieve the results. This entails changes in the way managers and hourly employees (referred to henceforth as "employees") are evaluated and rewarded.

We will discuss three main areas of current practice:

a. Employee performance measurement.
b. Employee performance remedies.
c. Employee rewards, financial and non-financial.

a. Employee performance measurement

What is it and why is it important?

Value streams require a culture of continuous improvement. Specific measurements are used within the cells and the value stream as a whole to make sure this is happening as planned. See chapter C.1 for a detailed discussion of performance measurement for the value stream and cells.

Performance measurements for the people within the value stream must refer to this context. But the measurements that will keep the value stream flowing, or that will keep the cells within the value stream working to takt time, or will keep the whole value stream performing toward goals in accordance with policy-- these measurements are not useful for evaluating individual employees.

Traditional MBO (Management by Objectives) systems reward employees who achieve their objectives, targets, quotas, personal goals, or results; these form the basis for employee and management appraisal systems in common use at many companies. Appraisals are calibrated on how well the manager or employee performed during the appraisal period in meeting targeted results. To achieve high ratings employees and managers must meet their agreed-upon targets. Little attention is paid in most traditional appraisal systems to sustain a problem-solving culture. It is not an overstatement to say that it's nearly impossible to create the lean culture without changing management and employee appraisal systems.

What are the negative impacts?

Lean requires the active involvement of management in the problems of employees. On the other hand, MBO-based appraisal systems imply that it is not necessary for a manager to get directly involved in solving their employees' problems meeting targets. Achieving the numerical target is the goal, and if you achieve it you are a good "manager" and a bad one if you do not. Managers who are rewarded based upon results alone usually rely upon exhortations to make employees work harder and smarter. Such appraisal systems give the manager little incentive to get directly involved in the in the work itself, to identify root causes for problems, and to implement improvements that foster success for all.

Frequently managers in such system do not understand the work sufficiently well to help employees remove obstacles that cause poor results, such as poorly maintained tooling or machines, fuzzy definitions of what constitutes acceptable workmanship, inadequate or no training in how to perform the work, poor incoming quality or missing components from suppliers to the operation.

Typical and recurring complaints from employees indicate the nature of the problems they have:

1. Supervisors or foremen who don't understand the work.
2. Inadequate training in their jobs.
3. Shortage of components at their work station.
4. Poor documentation of how to do the job.
5. Out of date engineering drawings.
6. Expedited or last-minute orders.
7. Inadequate or lost tooling.
8. Inability to get help from engineers.

Most of these problems are outside the control of the employee to solve on his own. He needs the active intervention of management.

These symptoms are only exacerbated by management appraisal systems that focus on financial or business results. Such systems reward detached management and create disincentives to get involved with finding the root causes that underlie poor results. Performance appraisal systems that are based on achieving results or quotas must be eliminated.

 Lean is a people system. Everyone is responsible. Everyone is on the team. Power that is shared is empowering.

To achieve numerical or financial results, employees are given numerical quotas or targets that they have to achieve. Typically, these follow a well-constructed management by objectives linkage. This emphasis has the effect of penalizing employees who stop to fix problems as they occur in the interest of higher quality. It rewards employees who get the work out, whether the quality is good or bad. In this way it forces employees to bury their pride of workmanship and causes them to become discouraged and negative toward their work. Quota-based systems have no place in a manufacturing environment that strives to achieve a problem-solving culture.

Some of the undesirable effects of non-lean performance appraisal systems are:

1. They have the effect of fostering a competitive environment among people and functions that need to work together in order to achieve overall value stream effectiveness;
2. They tend to pit employees against each other;
3. They create barriers to teamwork necessary to lean;
4. They create an atmosphere of fear of losing their jobs, which stifles creativity;
5. They devalue people and their desire to do a good job;
6. They foster a management ethic of achieving results that alienates manager from employee and inhibits the development of a problem-solving and continuous improvement culture.

Appraisal and ranking systems based on individual achievement must be abandoned in favor of team-based value stream-oriented systems.

What does lean performance appraisal look like and how do you achieve it?

We use a multi-step process to transform the evaluation process:

Step 1: Eliminate MBO for management and employee appraisal systems. Substitute a model for management leadership that creates a focus on achieving lean/hoshin goals at all levels. Some examples of these goals are:

1. Value to customers
2. On time delivery to customer specifications
3. System quality
4. System productivity
5. System flow at rate of customer pull
6. Emphasis on employee empowerment
7. Emphasis on integrity and mutual respect

Step 2: Shift your appraisal process from employee evaluation to employee development. The goal here is to provide employees the means to eliminate obstacles that prevent achieving the lean/hoshin goals of the company. Here are examples of some of the management behaviors that will accomplish this.

1. Carefully select new hires based upon their suitability to thrive in a lean culture.
2. Clearly define employees' jobs and the skills involved.
3. Educate and train people so that they know their jobs.
4. Eliminate quotas and targets.
5. Use measurements of employee performance that serve to raise the performance levels of all employees in the team.
6. Provide special help for those who have difficulty gaining the skills to perform the tasks required by standard work.
7. Use PDCA problem solving methods (described in Chapter C.1) to identify and eliminate obstacles to employees' doing quality work.
8. Create incentives and reinforcement for employees who make positive changes in the workplace that they can do without expending company resources.

You must create a culture that empowers and respects employees. Some things you can do to encourage this:

1. Enforce a code of conduct.
>   For example, one company used a code of conduct that required that employees do the following:

>   1. Respect others
>   2. Tell the truth
>   3. Be fair
>   4. Try new ideas
>   5. Ask why
>   6. Keep your promises
>   7. Do your share

Everyone in the company had to follow to the code. Anyone could be challenged, including managers. Violations led to probation and a supervisor corrective action plan. Repeated violations led to termination. Senior leadership in the company was required to exemplify the code.

2. Encourage continuous improvement.
>   Do this by:

>   1. Providing training for all team members
>   2. Working with the teams to select some short term, high success projects
>   3. Providing time and mentoring to the teams
>   4. Allowing the teams to be successful
>   5. Providing recognition
>   6. Having team members train new teams

3. Create a "no blame" environment.
>   It must be safe to reveal errors, mistakes, and problems through a formal mechanism for solving problems. One way of doing this is to

use a method called the "top and bottom 10 percent method." Here's how it works:

1. Managers are asked to identify the top and bottom 10% of all associates. They are directed to use the following criteria: communication, teaming, decisions, flexibility, resourcefulness, strategic thinking, analytical skills, technical competence and leadership.
2. The top 10% are considered future leaders and are given opportunities to develop through job rotation and leadership training.
3. The bottom 10% work with the manager to identify specific areas of improvement and develop an action plan.

4. Provide coaching and mentoring.

Avoid direct or punitive correction; use questioning and active listening. What you want to create is a learning environment where people learn by doing. If you tell people the "solution" every time, they will not learn, and your solution may not be the best solution.

5. Conduct employee attitude surveys.

These need to be concise and easy-to-use. They need to be aimed at identifying problems in associate-supervisor and associate-management relationships. The survey should focus on overall employee satisfaction with the workplace and the benefits program. It should be completely confidential. After the survey results are tabulated, the company president and/or executive team need to sit with each team and discuss the issues and problems identified. They should take action on the issues, or explain why they can't. It is important to couple survey results with leadership development action plans.

6. Encourage employee suggestions and reward the team for submitting suggestions.

7. Standardize work for leaders.

Doing this brings the following benefits: consistent leadership and management; continuity of best practice; minimal variability; disciplined lean operations; clear definition of what's expected of a leader; sets up average leaders for success. Additionally, it ensures leadership training and mentoring of employees; enables leaders to be successful; focuses on the "right things" such as serving the customer; helps maintain standardized work in production and administrative processes; ensures continuous improvement.

Develop team leaders' standardized work around maintaining production to takt time, ensuring standardized work is being followed, and creating local improvement.

Develop supervisors' standardized work around monitoring and supporting the team Leads to follow their standardized work.

Build value stream managers' standard work to support the supervisors' efforts to maintain their standard work.

b. Employee performance correction.

Step 3: When there is a performance problem, apply tools that help define what action is needed. The following example is adapted from the window-analysis method used in CEDAC (see Fukuyama, Ryuji "CEDAC, A Tool for Continuous Systematic Improvement" Productivity Press, Portland, Oregon, 1986)

		Standard Work	
		Known	**Not Known**
Standard Work	**Practiced**	**Case A:** Ideal State	**Case C:** Standard work has been established but some people who should know the procedure have not been informed
	Not Practiced	**Case B:** Standard work has been established but there is someone who does not practice the procedures correctly (three situations)	**Case D:** Adequate standard work has not been established

Figure 65. Example analysis of employee standard work problems

In the example above we have two scenarios related to standard work:

1. *Either it has been communicated and is known by individuals performing the work or it is not*

2. *Either it is practiced by people performing the work or it is not*

It is important that management takes the time to identify the root causes of employee problems. There are three cases which might prevail. Continuing with our example in Figure 64 above, these are shown in Figure 66.

Case		Problem Description	Possible Countermeasure
B	Situation 1	Although the correct method is known, there are careless mistakes, resulting in non adherence to procedure	Create mistake proofing
	Situation 2	Although the correct method is known, someone lacks the skills and cannot use the knowledge	Skill training, visual posting
	Situation 3	Although the correct method is known, lack of time, manpower, adequate tools leads to non adherence to procedure	Remove the obstacles that cause non-adherence
C		Adequate standard work has been established but some people who should know the procedure have not been informed	Training in the standard work, visual posting
D		Adequate standard work has not been established	Create new standard work

Figure 66. Employee problems and countermeasures

When a problem is identified, it is important to discover whether it resulted from a lack of adequate standard work, the employee's failure to understand the standard work, carelessness, or issues outside the employee's control, for example involving machinery, incoming materials, or tooling. The CEDAC framework, combined with PDCA problem solving, forms the basis for sorting out what appropriate action should be.

Active involvement by management in the application of this method will ensure that a continuous improvement process is sustained and that the process of employee evaluation is transformed in a way that supports lean.

c. Lean employee rewards -- financial and non-financial

Lean requires a strong team orientation. The relevant team is the value stream or plant; it is important that everyone in the value stream or plant is rewarded for success when value stream goals are achieved.

There are two types of rewards we can consider: *financial and non-financial.*

Financial rewards

The following guidelines are suggested:

1. Link the rewards to achievement of the hoshin goals of the value stream.
2. Eliminate performance ranking as the basis for establishing pay raises and profit sharing.
3. Provide equal pay raises and profit sharing to all persons in the value stream.

These guidelines, combined with the changes in employee performance measures will align the incentives of the individual with those of the company and create a system that will help focus the individual on maximizing customer value.

Non-financial rewards

Using non-financial rewards provides another way to recognize and reinforce lean behaviors that have helped achieve value stream goals. Examples of reasons why such rewards would be offered might include:

1. Participation rate of the team and achievement
2. Number of improvement projects
3. Cross training accomplishments
4. Use of standard process

Examples of non-financial rewards include:

1. Awards
2. Site presentations
3. Time off
4. Special lunch or recognition dinner
5. Chartered teams
6. More autonomy & authority

E1: Internal Accounting Controls

Background and definitions -- why this is important

Section 404 of the Sarbanes-Oxley Act of 2002 requires managements of publicly traded companies to conduct an annual assessment of the effectiveness of internal accounting controls related to the integrity of their financial statements. It is required that this assessment be reviewed by the company's external auditors. Assessment guidelines are laid out in the 1992 report of the Committee of Sponsoring Organizations of the Treadway Commission (COSO.) Because lean manufacturing has so significant an effect on the internal control environment, we must consider how this affects lean accounting methods.

Users of this toolkit may not be familiar with internal accounting control concepts. So here are some definitions and some background on the ways that lean manufacturing affects accounting control.

The 1992 report of COSO set forth a common definition of internal control and provided a standard process that businesses should use to evaluate their internal control systems. COSO defined internal control as: "a process designed to provide reasonable assurance about achieving objectives in the following categories:

1. Effectiveness and efficiency of operations.
2. Reliability of financial reporting.
3. Compliance with applicable laws and regulations."

Within each category the COSO report defined five interrelated components:

1. The Control environment—the atmosphere in which people conduct their activities, establishing the control tone of the organization.

2. Risk assessment—the identification and analysis of risks to the achievement of operations, financial reporting and compliance objectives, at the strategic, process and activity levels. The COSO report identified two types of risks: failure to achieve objectives and material misstatement of the financial statements. In analyzing these risks the COSO report specifies an analytical framework that includes the significance (or materiality) of the amount at risk, the likelihood of occurrence, and actions the entity takes to manage the risk.

3. Control activities—the policies, procedures and structures that help ensure necessary actions are taken to address risks to achieving the entity's objectives. The COSO report provided examples of traditional control activities such as review of performance measurement reports, physical control of assets, reconciliations of detailed transactions to totals, information processing edits, and segregation of duties.

4. Information and communication—the way information is identified, captured and communicated in form and time frame that enables people to carry out their responsibilities.

5. Monitoring the internal control system—the internal control systems must be monitored regularly to ensure they are relevant and operating as planned.

How lean manufacturing improves operating control

Lean manufacturers take a fundamentally different approach to managing risk from traditional internal accounting control.

Traditional control activities rely on review and inspection of transactions and results against a standard followed by correction of the errors that resulted from the deviations. Think: "auditing."

In contrast, lean controls work to prevent errors in the first place by building control into the structure of the work itself. Think: "prevention."

When an error does occur, lean manufacturers aggressively seek the root cause and implement error-proofing strategies so that the mistake never happens again. A lean control strategy is designed to perfect the system, not merely to correct errors generated repeatedly from a defective system. Traditional control activities are too cumbersome and unfocused to be useful in a lean company for the following reasons:

1. They happen too long after the fact to be helpful.
2. They fix the effects of problems but not the underlying causes.
3. They generally have long feedback loops that are disconnected from underlying root causes
4. They are time-consuming and costly and do not provide any value to the customer; lean would define them as waste.

Lean companies use consistently applied disciplines, continuous improvement, mistake proofing and standardized processes to control production, reduce inventory, stabilize quality and reduce manufacturing lead times.

Summary of lean controls

1. Minimize probability of errors and misstatements by means of:
   a. 5S and visual controls
   b. Standard work, standard (takt) time, standard inventory
   c. Hourly/by shift variance analysis of adherence to standard—work, time, and inventory at cell
   d. Culture of problem identification and solving
   e. Mistake proofing (poka yoke) devices or strategies
   f. Weekly feedback at the value stream—productivity, quality, delivery, cost

2. Reduce size (materiality) of amounts at risk by implementing:
   a. Short lead times—low and level inventory
   b. Visual pull/kanban system caps inventory quantity—assures low inventories
   c. Production stops to fix problems—little problems don't grow to be big problems
   d. Regular sales and operations planning drives establishment of kanban and takt—capacity is balanced to meet planned demand

Examples of lean controls and the risks they are designed to mitigate

Lean control	Risk that is mitigated
Use a kanban to pull from upstream operations based on what you need.	Poor communication in production scheduling. Lean companies make only based on a customer order and use simple visual communications such as a kanbans to signal the need to start production. Information is not hidden in a computer but is available for all to see.
Upstream operation only makes what is pulled.	Occurrence of obsolete inventory. Because lean companies only make what has been ordered, there is little risk inventory that cannot be sold will accumulate.
	Occurrence of damaged products in storage. Lean companies maintain very low work in process inventories and finished goods inventories and these inventories turn rapidly. They are able to do this as a result of changes on the shop floor such as reducing changeover times, eliminating quality problems and only making what has been ordered as signaled by a kanban.
	Improper shipments to customers. Lean companies make and ship to customer orders and have short lead times due to the need to have large amounts of work in process inventory to run manufacturing.
Count cell level inventory (number of kanbans in front of cell, in the cell and after the cell) every shift and compare with planned level.	Inventory builds up, causing inventory control and flow to break down. This can happen because the flow has been disrupted for reasons such as: the kanban controls have not been not adhered to; there is a lack of parts; or a machine has broken down, causing inventory to accumulate. When this happens the problems are immediately identified and fixed so that the proper flow in the cell can be resumed. From a financial point of view, this greatly strengthens control over inventory levels.
Order only from certified suppliers.	Poor supplier performance. Lean companies make it a practice to order from suppliers they have certified. This control reduces the risk of supplier errors reflected in wrong shipments, poor quality, invoice errors and the like.
Use master POs and kanban to pull daily from suppliers only what is needed for the next day's production.	The occurrence of purchasing mistakes. Lean companies that use kanban methods to signal the need for materials from suppliers eliminate the possibility for errors in purchase orders for every demand placed on suppliers.
	Improper pricing on supplier invoices. Lean companies do not pay from supplier invoices, but instead from the information on master purchase orders and production completion documents. The quantity demanded is controlled by the kanban and the purchase cost is established by a master purchase agreement with the supplier. By improving purchasing control, many lean companies have been able to eliminate supplier invoices entirely and to pay from a receiving or production completion document.
Create a culture of identifying problems and stopping production to fix them.	Improper quantity and wrong items manufactured. Lean companies measure the amounts manufactured hourly compared with plan at each major cell (or group of operations) and work to identify and fix the root causes of any deviation. That way, problems in meeting planned deliveries are identified early in the day so that effective counter-measures can be applied.
	Occurrence of scrap and rework. Rigorous attention is paid to performing work to standardized procedures. Workers in a downstream operation will not accept an item from an upstream operation that contains a defect. Defects that are discovered create a cause to stop production and fix the problem causing the defect. Therefore, the impact of a defect-causing problem is not perpetuated beyond one item. Quality is measured hourly and deviations subjected to the most rigorous scrutiny.

Lean companies make the effort to focus single-mindedly on such controls. As a result they have been able to eliminate wasteful activities in manufacturing, such as expediting, stock handling/clerking, scheduling, quality inspection, and the like. And consequently they have drastically reduced the risk of errors and mistakes that would cause misstatements in the financial reports. All the while, they are able to maintain high quality.

Strategies that lean companies use for reducing the significance of the amounts at risk...
(and thereby reducing the impact of errors that could occur undetected)

1. They produce very small batches, sometimes only one piece at a time, ensuring that the impact of mistakes will be limited only to the small number of items in the small batch, not to a whole shift's production as can happen in traditional manufacturing systems.
2. They have very low inventories, reducing the impact of mistakes in inventory balances.
3. They have small individual supplier orders, reducing the amounts owed to a supplier on any given receipt of raw material, and thereby minimizing the potential impact of an error on raw material inventory and accounts payable.
4. They ship in smaller quantities, reducing the accounts receivable from a customer on any given shipment. Consequently, the potential impact of an error on finished goods inventory and accounts receivable is consistently low.

In summary, lean controls reduce both the risk and the significance of potential errors and misstatements, in terms of the COSO framework.

	Low	Medium	High
High	None	Monitor, Take Action to Mitigate	Monitor, Take Action to Mitigate
Medium	None	Monitor	Monitor, Take Action to Mitigate
Low	None	None	None

Figure 67. Lean controls reduce both the risk and materiality of misstatements

This type of improved control environment allows lean companies to replace their traditional transaction-based systems without losing control of the business. Examples of such eliminated transactions include:

1. Eliminating work orders and production tracking documents.
2. Eliminating purchase orders to suppliers.
3. Eliminating supplier invoices.
4. Not valuing immaterial work in process inventory.
5. Moving to process costing based on value streams.

The best lean companies record only two transactions: the receipt of the customer order and the shipment of the product. All other transactions within the plant are considered unnecessary and are eliminated.

a. Including accounting controls on value stream or process maps

How do I do it?

Sarbanes documentation following the COSO requirements requires management to develop a matrix of risks and mitigating controls coupled with process maps showing how the controls impact the accounting process. This fits in well in a lean environment; lean production relies to a great extent on visual controls.

It makes lean sense to include accounting controls on the value stream and process maps. The company is already using them to define and configure current and future operations.

The best way to do this is for the financial team to participate in value stream and process mapping. This ensures that accounting control will progress in sync with evolving production processes. We use a four-step procedure, as follows:

1. Create a control matrix for the current state on a large piece of paper. Make sure you include each of the processes drawn on the value stream map. Your matrix will define 2 elements for each process:
   1) the control risk(s) for each process and
   2) the control methods that address the risks.
2. Write a Post-It® for each control method and stick it on the map with its process.
3. Operations might object to putting accounting controls on its map. The finance team can use a duplicate.
4. Post the controls map alongside the operations map.

Use the same procedure to map controls for the planned future state.

As improvements happen in operations, revisit your current state accounting controls matrix. Keep it up to date with new Post-Its.® The finance team must make sure that controls over the process are adequate to manage risks at all times during the lean transformation.

> Use Post-Its® on the value stream map at the control points. This gives you a visual way to show your accounting control architecture and make sure it relates well to production.

Here are examples of how accounting controls are overlaid on value stream maps.

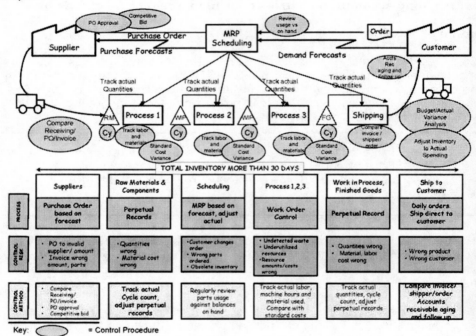

Figure 68. Current state map with controls matrix

Notice that the matrix below the map includes each operating process and inventory from the value stream map. You see all the accounting/control processes that accompany each operation (in ovals on the map) and the associated risks and control methods (in boxes beneath the map.)

Next you carry these concepts into the future.

Here's an example of the same value stream, but in its planned future state.

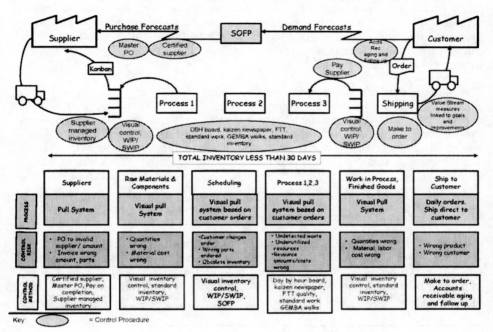

Figure 69. Planned future state map with controls matrix

As a result of lean manufacturing improvements, here's what happened:
Current state:

1. Production lead time is about 6 weeks.
2. Expediting happens frequently.
3. WIP inventory varies considerably
4. Production costs vary considerably.

Future state:

1. Production lead time is 2.5 days.
2. Cycle times are predictable; one every 6 minutes.
3. WIP is low and consistent.
4. Processes and costs are under control.
5. Operational performance measurements are working.
6. The continuous improvement team constantly works to improve the value stream.

The contrast between current and planned future state controls is visually clear.

The current state processes are transaction-based and controls are tailored to that environment. A lot of attention and work is dedicated to making sure the postings are accurate; authorizations for transactions and limits are in place; proper documentation for payments to suppliers exists; assets and liabilities are properly valued. The control philosophy is to inspect and reconcile, to make sure transactions have been processed correctly. Errors would typically be found long after the fact.

The planned future state approach emphasizes developing operations processes that are inherently in control. This means that the accounting control objectives are embedded in the structure of the operations processes themselves. When errors happen, they happen in a controlled environment, where the risks to the integrity of the financial systems are understood and are minimal by design. Errors are usually found quickly. The value stream team (always in pursuit of perfection) will work to eliminate the root causes. Gradually errors will disappear and control will improve.

b. Transaction elimination matrix

Getting rid of wasteful transactions without losing control of the business is at the heart of making lean manufacturing succeed. The challenge for chief financial officers, controllers, and their external auditors at companies implementing lean manufacturing is to develop a plan for adapting the internal accounting controls.

Question: When can a lean company eliminate old transaction-based controls?
Answer: When you can prove the new controls are in place and working as planned.

What does it do and why use it?

The transaction elimination matrix provides a structured way to progress from traditional transaction-based accounting with standard costing to value stream based accounting using direct costing. The matrix allows you to develop a plan that can then be reviewed and approved by management and internal and external auditors.

The matrix identifies trigger points, i.e. "what must be in place" from a lean perspective, to permit modifications to internal controls. This approach enables objective review of the process (has a trigger point been met?) before changing the way the process is controlled.

The transaction elimination matrix is a visual tool for making change happen in a clearly understood way. The risks involved are understood and plans for minimizing or eliminating these risks are in place.

Here are the steps we use:

BMA Inc. The Lean Accounting Leaders

Step 1: develop your own matrix.

We have created a "starter set" you can use as a model. In it, we suggest you track change through the five stages of lean maturity (or maturity path), which are:

1. Making a start with lean
2. Lean pilots in place
3. Lean production
4. Value stream management
5. Lean enterprise

Your company may already have other assessment tools that define the maturity path for lean manufacturing. If you can, use the same categories from the lean manufacturing assessment.

Create a matrix with the categories of lean across the top and typical categories of lean initiatives that affect the control of the process down the left side, such as:

1. Value stream cycle time
2. Inventory levels
3. Kanban and pull
4. Standard work
5. Supplier quality
6. Cell quality
7. Performance measures
8. Visual systems
9. Engineering data
10. Organization and control

Figures 70 and 71 represent our suggested "Starter Set."

The first two pages show where you are and where you plan to end up in these key lean categories. The third page (Figure 71) maps out the transactions that can be eliminated, and correlates these to the maturity path.

Please take this as just an example and do not copy it verbatim. A primary value of the Transaction Elimination Maturity Path is in the development of the content along with a cross-functional team from finance, operations, lean specialists, auditors, etc.

Category	Making a start with lean	Lean pilots in place	Value streams in place	Lean value stream management	Lean enterprise
Production Flow Time	• 12 week lead time • No lean concept • Huge batch sizes	• 5 week lead time • Value streams starting to be mapped • Start creating flow in assembly cells	• 3 to 4 week lead time • Bottlenecks identified	• 3 days • Cells continue to shorten cycle time • All production is linked to customer takt time.	• 3 day • Supplier is linked to customer takt time • 100% customer service level.
Inventory Levels	• 2 turns • High raw, WIP and finished goods inventories • While inventories are high it's not the right stuff.	• 2 turns • Using kanbans • High non-performing obsolete inventory	• 5 turns • Kanban is used to pull from all internal areas • Visual systems • Supermarkets being used • Consistent level of inventory at point of use.	• 20 turns • Kanban pull from customer • Most inventory at point of use	• 40 turns end of year • 30 turns mid-year • Supplier making milk runs and monitoring inventory levels • VMI for our customers
Kanban and Pull	• MRP • Push System • No kanban pull	• Introducing kanban in cells • Kanban with some suppliers • Pull system used in assembly cells • VMI in place • Still over producing	• Pull system in all areas of organization • Pull system with all suppliers • Fewer batch jobs • Smaller batch sizes • Set-up time reduction being worked on	• 1 piece flow or equivalent • Kanban throughout • Levelized schedule • Supplier kanban on most items.	• 1 piece flow or equivalent. • Customer pull from us • Ability to deliver directly to customer's
Standard Work	• Using routings for standard costing	• Started 5-S • Assembly cells are balanced • Workers are being cross trained	• Start using visual work instructions • Start standard work for all cells • Cross training program in place	• Paperless • Standard work across value stream including non production areas • Lean team monitors performance	• Visual systems • Continuous improvement • Line balancing based on customer takt time.
Supplier Quality	• Many suppliers but few are certified • Frequent supplier delivery problems • Receiving inspects most incoming material • Inspection shows erratic supplier quality	• Identified core suppliers • Decreased the number of suppliers. • Have some certified suppliers • No longer inspect receipts from certified suppliers	• 75% of core suppliers are certified • Certified suppliers delivering 80% direct to point of use • Most, if not all, other suppliers are certified • Frequent deliveries using kanbans • Measuring suppliers as responsible for quality • Develop supplier certification program	• Moving to six sigma • All certified suppliers address quality issues • Value stream manages the inventory • Material is delivered directly to point of use • Certified suppliers are lean too	• Six sigma • Customer is involved with supplier quality • All suppliers are lean • All suppliers are certified

Figure 70. Transaction elimination: what must be in place.

Category	Making a start with lean	Lean pilots in place	Value streams in place	Lean value stream management	Lean enterprise
Cell Quality	• Large batches • Scrap rework issues • Only 75% on time delivery to next operation	• Formed assembly cells • Using pull system in some areas • Smaller batches • There is better quality and less rework.	• Single piece flow • Identifying root cause on quality issues/correct • Operators inspect • Time to stop and fix	• Moving to six sigma • Quality is part of the process • Mistake proofing processes ("Poka yoke") • All inspection outside of cells has been eliminated	• Six sigma quality
Performance measures	• Using detailed labor reports for efficiency • Using machine utilization measures • Measures are primarily accounting	• Use white boards • Tracking hourly production • Using traditional measurements for decision making	• Start using lean performance measures. e.g. scrap, day-by-hour, 1st time through and other lean performance measures. • Running to takt day-by-hour report • Have a uniform measurement system for all cells	• Value stream measurements • Cell measurements that are linked to the value stream measures.	• Cell measures and value stream measures are integrated with strategic goals • Continuous process of using measures to refine and improve.
Visual systems	• No visual systems. It is basically, paper, paper and more paper. • MRP work orders, and Ad hoc reports are used.	• Measure boards in cells. • Measures posted real time(sometimes) • Display is simple to understand	• Line of sight • Measure boards are by value stream. • Kanban pull signals	• Visual systems used throughout value stream. • Pull system triggered by customer orders (kanban)	• Customer tied in to supplier. • Manage the customer order.
Engineering data	• Have multiple level bills of material • Routings and bill of materials are inaccurate	• Bills of material and process sheets are simple • Engineering responsible to keep BOM and routings accurate	• Cell personnel participate in concurrent engineering and process reviews • Cell takes appropriate actions to update the requirements	• Bill of material and routings are maintained by value stream. continuous improvement team • Paperless.	• Information flows from customer to us to supplier. • Improvements by continuous improvement teams.
Organization and control	• Organized by department	• Started learning about Value Streams	• Value streams clearly identified with some allocations and some direct costing. • Cross functional training • Addressing compensation structure for alignment. • Matrix management	• All functions are in the value stream. • Organized and managed by value stream. • Support functions within value stream. • Measures by value stream.	• Suppliers and customers are included in the value streams.

Figure 70-b. Transaction elimination: what must be in place. (contd..)

Category	Making a start with lean	Lean pilots in place	Lean production	Lean value stream management	Lean enterprise
Eliminate Labor reporting	• Since labor is small % of total product costs, there is some backflushing and/or elimination of labor reporting. • Many units will still use detailed labor reporting.	• Some backflushing of labor • Detailed labor records are starting to go away.	• For pay purposes, either salaried workforce or exception based reporting for hours • For cost purpose, all labor(direct and indirect) is charged to the value stream.	• Exception based reporting minimized to labor law requirements	• Non exempt salary workforce
Eliminate production tracking and Inventory	• Backflushing some material • Still cycle counting for inventory problems	• Eliminate receiving stock withdrawal tickets and associated moves bys canning parts in at receiving (supplier will stock be barcode) • Developing plans for Kanban process	• Full pull system • Scrap-exceptions. • Supplier managed inventories • Low value multiple use stock to be expensed when purchased.	• Inventories are minimized • Eliminate cycle counting • No stockroom transactions • Stock is delivered to point of use	• Complete pull system from customer through supplier. • Everything is period cost.
Eliminate Requisitions, Purchase Orders, Receiving and AP	• Have blanket PO's with release schedule. • Implementing ERS to eliminate invoices and 3-way match. • Implementing P Cards for low dollar non-inventory purchases • Implementing EDI purchasing • Set up long term agreements	• Eliminate some PO's with pull system. • Autoplay; no more invoicing and/or 3 way match. • Eliminate some PO releases by having kanban system. • No longer receive invoices • Web based purchasing • More ERS as suppliers are certified • More P cards • Beginning a pull system with supplier and have fewer monthly releases. • Expanding Web based purchasing	• Backflush inventory and pay by backflush • Eliminate receiving function. • No PO's since full pull system • Increase P card usage to inventory items (low value) • Supplier managed inventories • Initial blanket PO with no updates. Suppliers will be triggered electronically due to Kanban. • Backflushing based on shipments.	• Initial blanket PO for each Part no. with annual review of pricing. • Purchasing group engineering group and accounting group are all part of the value stream. • Pay by backflush	• Eliminate accounts payable function because of limited amount of checks to cut. • Eliminate receiving with suppliers delivering to point of use.

Figure 71. Transactions to eliminate

This type of matrix helps create a controlled migration strategy from the current state to the planned future state in parallel with changes being made in operations. The key issue is understanding what has to be in place from a lean point of view so control processes can be eliminated while still keeping the business under control.

Use these four major steps:

1.Understand what lean controls will be planned and when.

When planning the lean manufacturing environment, sit down with the operations managers and go over their plans. Assist operations in preparing pages one and two of the matrix if this has not already been done. Use the Starter Set" to guide you. Ask questions, such as:

1. When will cell-level measurements be implemented?
2. What will be inventory turns at each stage of implementation? When will work-in-process inventories be low and level? What are the planned error-proofing devices and what is the expected improvement in resulting quality?
3. When will pull and kanban systems be in place? What will be their impact on inventory turns and product lead times? When will work-in process inventories be low and level? When will finished goods inventories be low and level?
4. When will all major suppliers be certified? When will master purchase orders be used instead of individual orders for each purchase? When will kanban/pull systems be used to procure raw materials? When will suppliers begin delivering raw materials to the production line

instead of to raw materials stores?

5. When will production be initiated from a customer order rather than from a work order?

6. When will lean performance measurements drive the work of continuous improvement?

2. Understand which traditional controls can be eliminated as lean is introduced.

First you have to understand why the existing controls are in place and what risks they protect against. This involves analyzing each control and the related lean manufacturing control that will replace it. Accountants and auditors should use this knowledge to develop a plan to phase in new controls as lean manufacturing progresses.

 Lean manufacturing classes are not just for operations people! Finance people have to acquire the language of lean and understand lean methods. Go ahead! Take a class.

Generally there is a progression, or "maturity path," that is followed. Here is an example on the subject of work orders:

Lean manufacturing stage	Work order processes
You are making a start with Lean	You track all transactions (inventory, labor, etc.) to jobs through work orders.
Lean pilots are in place	You eliminate detailed job step tracking and backflush using standard costs for actual production to the work order as cells are implemented. Track only starts and completions. (Note: "backflushing" is a costing method that uses standard material quantities and labor hours included in the standard costs to charge costs of production to a work order. It eliminates the need for tracking "actual" labor hours and materials used in production).
Lean production is working in the plant	You backflush to the work order using larger portions of the manufacturing process, such as from fabrication or assembly. Or, you backflush from completions all the way through the production process.
You are managing by value streams	You eliminate backflushing altogether and charge costs directly to a value stream general ledger account as they are incurred. Eliminate work orders.

Here's an example of what must be in place for tracking material and labor through production:

Steps	Actions	What Controls Must be in Place
1	Eliminate job step tracking. Track only starts and completions	Accurate labor routings and bills of materials
2	• Eliminate detailed tracking • Automate the assignment of labor/material through backflushing using standard labor costs and actual production—backflush to work order	Accurate labor routings and bills of materials
3	• Backflush Overhead based on ratio of value stream indirect to direct to work order • Eliminate detailed tracking and variance reporting	Cell level performance measures in place in pilot cells and day by the hour reporting in all work areas
4	Eliminate work order or other production tracking documents	• Extensive use of kanbans and visual systems • Standard work
5	Apply labor and overheads as summary direct costs to the value stream. Do not apply these costs to specific products or production jobs.	• Value Streams defined • Inventories low and consistent (over 12 turns) • Well-functioning kanban control • Level production demand • Processes under control

Figure 72. What must be in place example # 1

119

EI: b. Transaction Elimination Matrix

Steps	Actions	What Controls Must be in Place
1	The annual physical inventory is replaced with cycle counting. Cycle counting is used as a way to discover the root causes of errors created in the inventory balances. This way, the company is gradually eliminating the error-causing problems in its processes	• Accurate labor routings and bills of materials • Accurate records for scrap and rework • Backflushing maintains the inventory balances for each item
2	Kanban control of inventory in the cells eliminates the need for cycle counting, inasmuch as there is visual control of all work in process and material inventories at the lean cells.	•Value Streams defined • Inventories low and consistent (over 12 turns) • Well-functioning kanban control • Level production demand •Processes under control
3	• Inventory tracking has been largely removed from the computer system • Inventory valuation calculated from the number of days of inventory within the value stream	• Cell level performance measures in place in that count WIP versus standard WIP each shift • Well functioning kanban control • Level production demand

Figure 73. What must be in place example #2

Give careful thought to the maturity paths for eliminating transactions in all major processes. Processes other than those in our examples would be purchasing and accounts payable, closing the books, approval of transactions, and the like.

The results of this analysis should then be aligned with the operations plans on pages one and two of the matrix and included in page three at the appropriate stage.

Cross reference the transaction elimination matrix to the value stream maps that contain the key controls.

3. Include internal and external auditors in your plan.

It is important to involve both internal and external auditors. Get their sign-off on the conditions under which the company can eliminate transaction controls. Review the strength of the new controls before eliminating existing ones.

4. Monitor the effectiveness of the new control processes.

Periodically review with operations management how well the new controls are working. Build controls into the continuous improvement process.

Update the controls on the value stream maps as they are eliminated and replaced with new controls.

E2. Inventory Valuation

a. Simple methods to value inventory

Why use it?

As lean methods take hold within the company, inventory levels fall
dramatically. It is common for lean companies to see 50%-90% inventory
reductions. As inventory falls the value of the inventory become much
less significant; i.e. it represents much lower materiality. In addition, the
inventory comes under good control. This level of control is created by the
combination of low inventory, visual controls, pull systems with vendors, and
the responsibility for purchasing and inventory control residing within the value
stream team.

When inventory is low and under control simpler methods of inventory
valuation can be used.

1. Simpler inventory valuation methods are a lot less work.
2. Simpler inventory valuation methods do not require complex computer
   systems to track and maintain the information.
3. Simpler inventory valuation methods support and enhance visual
   inventory management.

How do I do it?

There are a number of common methods for valuing inventory. The most
simple can be used when inventory levels are very low and under clear
operational control. For example, a company that manufactures automotive
parts from blended powdered steel through a process of molding, sintering,
machining, finishing, packing, and shipping. The raw material is controlled
using vendor management inventory (VMI). The work in process is less than 2
days. Products are made to order and finished goods are never more than one
week waiting for shipment. The total inventory is 12-15 days and controlled
using lean supermarkets and pull systems. This company can value inventory
by a stock count and a simple inventory valuation calculation.

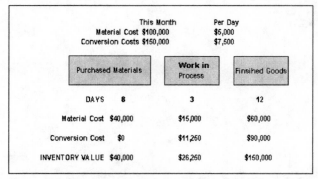

Figure 74. Simple method for calculating inventory value

Another company with a similar level of lean manufacturing capability making industrial valves has very low raw materials and low WIP, but must maintain relatively high finished goods to provide a high level of short lead time service to their customers. Simple methods can be used to value the raw material and WIP, but more complex methods are required for the finished goods because it is higher, and represents more significance.

Some common methods are:

1. Days of stock.

It is common for lean companies to track the number of days of inventory they hold in purchased materials, WIP, and finished goods. This is used as a performance measurement to gauge the rate of material flow through the value stream. When they have this information it is easy to calculate the inventory value. In the example below the material cost for the month in the value stream was $100,000 or $5,000 per day (in a 20 day month). The total conversion cost in the value stream was $150,000 or $7500 per day. If there are 8 days of purchase materials, then the valuation is 8*$5000 or $40,000. The value of 3 days of WIP comes to 3 days of material cost and 1.5 days of conversion cost - assuming the WIP items are half complete on average. The value of finished goods is 12 days of material cost and 12 days of conversion cost.

2. Material cost plus days of conversion cost.

Some companies keep track of the quantity of each item on the computer but track only material cost of their inventory. To value inventory they apply the conversion costs using the number of days. In the example above the material cost is already known to be a total of $115,000 and this is already reported on the balance sheet. At month end the controller needs to apply the conversion costs as a reversing journal entry to the balance sheet. There are 13.5 days of conversion cost to be applied; 12 days of finished goods and 1.5 days of WIP. The conversion cost that is debited to material on the balance sheet would be 13.5 * $7500 = $101,250.

3. Quantity of finished goods.

In companies that have large finished goods there are other methods to calculate finished goods value. Suppose the company above has 90 units of finished goods in stock and that during the month they have manufactured 150 units. The value of the finished goods inventory will be the total monthly value stream cost ($100,000 + $150,000) $250,000 multiplied by 90/150 = 0.6. This comes to $250,000 * 0.6 = $150,000

If instead of having 90 units of inventory the company had 190 units. This is more than the quantity manufactured this month - 150 units. In this case the finished goods inventory is valued at the total cost of the value stream for this month and 40/150 of the total cost of the prior month (if the prior months production quantity was also 150 units). The assumption is that the 150 made this month are all in finished goods inventory, together with 40/150 of the items manufactured during the prior month. These assumptions are true on average when the inventory is low, under control, and there is a pull system.

4. Average costs.

If we know that at the end of January the finished goods inventory is valued at $340,000 (for example) and we have manufactured 200 units during the month, then the average cost of a unit is $1,700. If the month-end stock is 90 units, then the value of the finished goods is:

90* $1,700 = $153,000

If the total number of units is more than one month's product, then this calculation is extended to include the average cost of the prior month, and perhaps the month before that.

5. Product cost.

If the company has larger finished goods inventories then the valuation will be more traditional. There are many companies that have become adept at lean methods within the production and have very low purchased materials and WIP, but maintain high finished goods because they are stored in warehouses in many different geographic locations. They need a method to value their inventory until they solve the problems causing the high inventory.

Under these circumstances it is necessary to track the quantity of finished goods on the computer systems and to maintain a product cost for each item. This is traditional except the product cost can be calculated using features and characteristics costing (F&C). F&C is usually simpler to calculate than a standard cost and is a more accurate number. It can be used for inventory valuation when there are high levels of stocks; until the company can solve the problems causing the high inventory. **See also section B.3.a. about features and characteristics product costing.**

6. Prior inventory plus purchases minus usage.

Another simple method for inventory value reporting is to take last month's value at material cost and add the amount of materials purchased this month, subtract the cost of materials scrapped during the month, subtract the material costs for the product shipped this month (from the bill of materials). This gives the material value of the inventory. The amount of conversion cost based upon the days of inventory is then added to give the total inventory value.

How do we know how much inventory we have?

Traditional companies hate physical inventory counts; yet they must do them. The whole operation takes several days to complete. It ties up resources to count, report, and reconcile the computer figures. It disrupts production. True, it may be of benefit to the auditors, but it is of no practical help to the company. In fact stock figures often seem to be less accurate after the stock count.

Many companies try to "solve" this by moving to regular cycle counting. Instead of a full annual stock count, the physical inventory is done little by little each week. More expensive items are counted more often than inexpensive commodities. These activities are of course 100% wasteful, but they satisfy the auditors and keep the balance sheet accurate.

Lean companies take the opposite approach. They eliminate the waste of cycle counting entirely. Instead, they move back to a full physical stock count; not annually but monthly or sometimes even weekly. The reason is that a full physical count in a lean company is quick and easy. When inventory is low and controlled visually it is very easy to count. Often it is not necessary to count the actual parts; you can just count the kanbans. The material and components are stored in standard containers with a standard kanban quantity in every container, and it is simple to count the number of containers or the number of kanban cards associated with them.

It is common for lean organizations to no longer track inventory on the computer system at all. If the visual control is robust and effective there is no need for a second, parallel tracking system.

What are the issues?

There are four issues to take account of when deciding about inventory valuation.

1. **The amount of inventory.** If the inventory is less than 30 days in total then simpler inventory valuation methods can be used. If the raw material and WIP inventory is less than 30 days and finished goods is higher; then simpler methods can be used for the raw materials and WIP. If the finished goods is under good control then it is possible to use the methods described above (quantity of finished goods or average costs.)

2. **Visual control.** If the inventory is under good visual control then it can be quick and easy to physically count the inventory and use these numbers for the inventory valuation using one of the methods given above.

3. **Tracking on the Computer.** If the stock quantities of each item are tracked on the computer system then we will know the number of each item we have in stock, and these numbers can be used to help value inventory. The usual reasons for tracking stock quantities on the computer include:
   -The need to provide control when the inventory is out-of-control and push-style replenishment systems are in use.

-There are too many part numbers for simple visual control.
-A need to see the on-hand balance quantities from a distance.
Sales people needing to access finished goods availability, for
example.

4. **The Inventory Mix is Different from the Sales Mix.** Most of the
   simpler methods of inventory valuation assume that the mix of items
   in inventory matches to the mix of products being made. The mix of raw
   materials and purchased components broadly matches the mix of those
   items being manufactured and sold. Similarly the mix of finished
   products is assumed to match the mix of products being manufactured.
   When this is not the case it is difficult to use the simpler inventory
   valuation methods. Lean manufacturing with small batches, single piece
   flow, and pull systems creates this matching. A company
   employing lean methods buy and manufacture what the customer is
   pulling. This - together with appropriate kanban calculations - ensures
   a good matching of inventory mix to sales.

Variations

1. **Excess and Obsolete Inventory.** Most companies go into lean
   methods with a certain amount of excess and obsolete inventory.
   These are usually caused by traditional batch production and
   purchasing methods. It is important when applying lean methods to
   physically segregate this inventory. If it obsolete then it should be
   disposed of. If it is excess to requirement then it can be treated like
   a "supplier". The pull system for the items pulls from the excess stock.
   Excess and obsolete inventory is addressed using 5S methods, i.e.:

   -*Sort* (identify the excess & obsolete materials)
   -*Set in Place* (locate excess away from the operational
    inventory and eliminate the obsolete)
   -*Shine* (maintain the excess inventory in an orderly and
    accessible manner)
   -*Standardize* (establish a pull system so the excess material is
    used over time)
   -*Sustain* (make sure the material can not be ordered from
    a supplier when there is excess!! Establish methods to
    prevent the generation of excess of other items)

2. **One-Time-Use Parts.** The methods described in this section are
   appropriate for the inventory valuation of regularly used production
   materials. When materials are low and under good visual operational
   control there is no need for the complex traditional inventory tracking
   and planning systems.

   Lean organizations that design-to-order will often need to purchase
   parts and materials that are used only once (or infrequently). These
   items often do not lend themselves to the simpler methods because
   they do not match the "low and under control" criteria. They are usually

maintained and valued in the traditional way, and may be purchased using an MRP method. If the value of these items is low they can be fully expensed at the time of receipt and disposed of rather than maintained on inventory. But in reality many of these one-time-use parts are quite expensive and need to tracked and controlled in detail.

Many lean organizations recognize the waste and confusion caused by these one-time-use items and work to reduce them by introducing design methods leading to the greater use of common parts wherever possible. But there will inevitably be items that must use the more complex methods. It is often possible, however, for 70%-90% of materials to be controlled and valued simply.

Getting started

As with all lean improvement the move towards simplified inventory valuation is not a one-time change-over.

Start with materials that are fast movers, that have certified suppliers, and that lend themselves to good visual control. These can be valued using the simplified methods and may be controlled without inventory tracking systems. Once these items are working well and the value stream teams have become skillful in lean methods, then these inventory valuation methods can be extended to other more difficult items.

Pulling it All Together

The Lean Business Management System

Why use it?

Why do so few companies complete the transformation to "lean enterprise"? Often they apply lean tools rigorously in their factories; they receive many benefits, but they don't change the way they manage or evaluate the business— exactly the change they need to make!

The lean business management system puts all the tools and methods of "lean manufacturing" and "lean accounting" together into a system that best manages and promotes a lean culture. Lean accounting supports lean operations by accurately reporting the financial impact of lean improvements in a way that is clear, understandable, and actionable. Lean accounting provides decision-making tools focused on lean value streams; it identifies areas where improvement projects will improve financial results, and it furnishes powerful planning tools for capacity requirements and much more.

In summary, the lean business management system allows managers to excel at lean.

Figure 75 on the below illustrates the entire set of lean business management methods and tools. We begin with learning lean methods and properly defining and mapping the value stream. For discussion purposes and planning, we break the tools and methods into the primary business functions: controlling, managing, planning, and improving. But bear in mind, what we are creating is an integrated system.

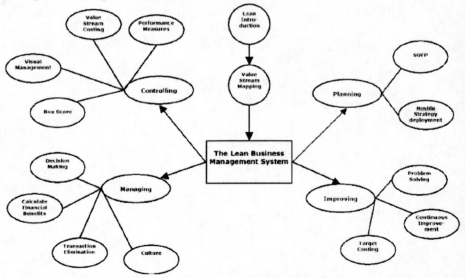

Figure 75. Tools and methods of value stream management

What does it do?

Value stream management builds and supports the lean enterprise.

 What is value stream management? It is standard work for leaders, who must manage value streams every day for customer value, continuous improvement, and long term prosperity.

Lean accounting has a crucial role to play. Finance and accounting people must live the five principles of lean thinking and understand lean manufacturing methods even better than the operational people. They are not just the accountants on the team. They are colleagues who focus on creating customer value, making continuous improvement happen day in and day out, and making more money.

How do I do it?

We use a five-step approach for creating the value stream management system.

Step 1: Defining the value stream.

This is the starting point for creating a lean management system. Issues to consider in Step 1 include:

1. Understanding how customer value is defined
2. Mapping the physical flow
3. Understanding how best to organize the value stream
4. Creating the value stream team
5. Understanding where the value is created
6. Identifying value and waste in the value stream
7. Focusing on value for the customer
8. Identifying flow and obstacles to flow
9. "Seeing" the issues and how to make improvements
10. Creating value, growth, and profit for the company

Step 2: Controlling the value stream.

This is the main work of the value stream team. Activities in Step 2 would include:

1. Implementing visually posted "Lean Performance Measures"
2. Using regular "gemba" walks for managing by looking, seeing and discussing and solving problems, and for managing the value stream team process itself.

Step 3: Managing the value stream.

Operational, financial and value stream capacity information is brought together to understand the impact of decisions on the value stream. Value stream income statements and box scores are tools that managers use to assess value stream performance and give employees and teams the information they need to succeed.

Step 4: Improving the value stream.

Relentlessly eliminate waste from all the processes of the value stream. Use the power of data from performance boards to drive improvements and create more value. Form a continuous improvement team empowered to implement breakthrough change or just-do-it improvements within the value stream. Always have a future state map and a transition plan to get there. Become excellent at using lean methods and tools.

Step 5: Planning the value stream

Lean planning is NOT the detailed, daily scramble of most traditional manufacturers. It is done monthly, integrated across value streams. It establishes production cycle times and level scheduling. It provides cross-functional coordination throughout the organization. It uses these lean tools:

1. Hoshin kanri strategy deployment
2. SOFP -- Sales operations and financial planning
3. Value stream cost and capacity analysis and box scores
4. Assessment of the financial impact of lean improvements

Value stream management is a key aspect of adopting "lean" as a business strategy. Top management must lead and support a lean transition for it to be sustainable and successful. Value stream management is the framework for leadership to follow as a company progresses down the maturity path to creating and managing lean culture in the organization.

This is not a quick fix! Lean is more than a collection of methods. It is the application of lean thinking to every aspect of the business. Lean companies are in it for the long haul, and the journey is never ending. And that's a good thing!

Lean accounting maturity path

What is it?

The maturity path for lean accounting is best route for successful implementation and sustainability of lean accounting. The maturity path constitutes the clear transition plan to a new system of measurement and control that replaces traditional control processes based upon mass production thinking.

Because lean accounting radically changes accounting, control and measurement processes, changes must be made prudently and carefully so control of the business is never lost.

Lean accounting can only happen when lean thinking and lean production methods are introduced and operational processes are brought under lean control. This eliminates the need for traditional control-by-transaction methods and opens the door to replacing them with lean accounting practices. The result of a successful implementation of lean accounting is a single system that combines operational and financial planning, reporting and control.

Why is it important?

Developing a maturity path is important because it is critical that operational and financial control be maintained. The traditional cost accounting controls do provide a means of controlling a business, even though these are not the proper controls for a lean company. It is unwise to stop using traditional cost accounting controls before new lean controls are put in place. The clear maturity path -- where lean accounting initiatives are clearly linked to lean manufacturing success -- ensures that control will be maintained.

How do I do it?

The first step in developing a lean accounting maturity path is to understand a typical maturity path for lean manufacturing. This breaks down into three distinct stages:

Stage 1 would typically have the following attributes: lean cells are in place, at minimum in pilots; there has been extensive lean training; flow and standardized work are being implemented.

Stage 2 is characterized by: management by value stream has been established; manufacturing in cells using standardized work and single piece flow is in wide use; there is extensive use of visual systems; there are fully functioning continuous improvement teams.

Stage 3 is characterized by: lean enterprise is in place, where the business is organized by value streams and lean thinking extends beyond the four walls of the factory to customers and suppliers.

The lean accounting maturity path will follow the lean manufacturing maturity path. The people in charge of a lean accounting implementation need to have an excellent understanding of how lean manufacturing matures and how to measure its success. The best way to do this is to have finance and accounting people on the lean team. They must fully participate in training and in continuous improvement planning and activities, such as kaizens. They must "learn by doing." The following table illustrates how the maturity paths of lean manufacturing and lean accounting correspond.

Lean manufacturing maturity path	Lean accounting maturity path
Pilot lean production cells	Getting started with lean accounting
Lean manufacturing is widespread	Managing by value stream
Lean thinking applied throughout company and partners	Lean enterprise

The next three tables illustrate how each lean accounting stage relates to the specific tools that support it.

Stage 1 -- Getting started with lean accounting. As lean production cells are put in place, a company needs to begin developing the box score data, begin transaction elimination and calculate the financial benefits of lean.

Lean accounting tools	Attributes
Box score -- performance measurements	1. Lean cell performance measurements should be implemented in all lean production cells. Additionally, visual management techniques should also be implemented. 2. Senior management should begin developing the lean performance measurement linkage chart: strategic measures, value stream measures and cell measures. 3. Lean performance measurements should be introduced throughout the company, especially in support and administrative processes.
Box score -- capacity	1. Current and future state value stream maps should be prepared for all value streams. 2. Initial calculation of value stream capacity (productive, nonproductive and available) should be completed.
Box score -- value stream costing	1. Using value stream maps, identify the drivers of value stream costs. 2. Begin assigning actual costs to value streams. 3. Identify the costs not assigned to any value stream. 4. Determine how to assign actual material cost to value streams.
Transaction elimination	1. Eliminate transactions from lean pilot cells through the introduction of back flushing material and eliminate labor reporting. 2. Stop variance analysis & reporting. Variances may still occur, but they "stay in finance." 3. Simplify standard costing by reducing the number of allocations and rates used. 4. Finance focuses on transaction elimination in all finance processes to create capacity for lean accounting initiatives.
Lean Decision Making	1. Begin using box score data to calculate the financial benefits of lean. 2. Illustrate how continuous improvement will improve performance measurements, eliminate nonproductive capacity and reduce costs. Then use simple scenarios projecting the financial impact of using freed up capacity to ship more orders to customers. Note -- it may also be necessary to model the financial impact of significant inventory reduction, which could be a short-term reduction in profits but an increase in cash flow.

Stage 2 -- Managing by Value Stream. As lean manufacturing becomes the operating system, it is critical that lean accounting practices take hold and replace traditional measurement, control and reporting practices.

Lean accounting tools	Attributes
Box score -- performance measurements	1. The lean performance measurement linkage chart becomes the primary method to control the operations. Strategic measures are reviewed monthly by senior management, value stream measures are used weekly by the value stream to plan & manage continuous improvement and cell measures are used on a daily basis to control cell production activities. 2. The lean performance measurement linkage chart has also been introduced into all support and administrative processes.
Box score -- capacity	1. The productive, nonproductive and available capacity of value streams is available weekly. 2. Value streams use the capacity analysis to plan & measure the impact of continuous improvement initiatives.
Box score -- value stream costing	1. Standardized work has been implemented so all costs are directly charged to value streams. 2. The general ledger is being modified for value stream costing. 3. A company value stream P&L can be produced that matches the traditional P&L. At a minimum it is used as an internal analysis tool, with the traditional P&L used for financial reporting. 4. Value stream P&L's are produced weekly for each value stream. 5. Features & Characteristics has been introduced to replace standard costing when a product cost is required.
Transaction elimination	1. Direct expensing of materials, labor and overhead costs to the value streams eliminates the need for most shop floor transactions and allocations. 2. Inventory tracking transactions are stopped, replaced by a pull system and visual management. 3. Procurement transactions such as individual purchase orders, receiving transactions and 3-way matching can be eliminated as supplier certification matures.
Planning and Budgeting	1. Monthly sales, operations and financial planning is used by value streams and senior management. 2. Budgeting is by value stream.
Lean Decision Making	1. Standardized processes have been created to analyze business decisions using box score data which considers the operational, financial and capacity impact of decisions. Examples of such decisions are make/buy, profitability of orders, capital purchases, outsourcing and new product profitability. 2. Standard costs are not used to make business decisions, even if standard costing is still required to value inventory.
Inventory Valuation	1. If standard costing is still required for inventory valuation, is it maintained only to value inventory and has been greatly simplified. 2. If inventory is low and consistent (30 days or less), simplified inventory valuation methodologies using value stream costing are introduced and standard costing is "turned off."

Stage 3 -- Lean Enterprise. As lean extends beyond the four walls of the factory and continuous improvement becomes a way of life, lean accounting has a key role in managing and controlling the business.

Lean accounting tools	Attributes
Box score -- performance measurements	1. The lean performance measurement linkage chart becomes the primary method to control the entire business.
Box score -- capacity	1. The productive, nonproductive and available capacity analysis has been extended into all support and administrative processes 2. All continuous improvement planning use the capacity analysis to plan & measure the impact of continuous improvement initiatives.
Box score -- value stream costing	1. The company value stream P&L has replaced the traditional P&L for financial reporting and is produced from the general ledger software system.
Transaction elimination	1. Two operational transaction occur -- receipt of materials and shipment of materials. 2. There is no tracking of materials or inventory in software systems.
Planning and Budgeting	1. Target costing is used in product and process design to link customer value to the business.
Lean Decision Making	1. Target costing is used to understand customer value and drive continuous improvement.
Inventory Valuation	1. Simplified inventory valuation methodologies using value stream costing are used. Inventory value is posted monthly using a journal entry.

List of Figures

BMA Inc. The Lean Accounting Leaders